the SUCCESS
CYCLE

the
SUCCESS
CYCLE

3 Keys for Achieving Your Goals in Business and Life

MARQUES OGDEN

Post Hill
PRESS

A POST HILL PRESS BOOK

The Success Cycle:
3 Keys for Achieving Your Goals in Business and Life
© 2020 by Marques Ogden
All Rights Reserved

ISBN: 978-1-64293-174-7
ISBN (eBook): 978-1-64293-175-4

Cover photo by Enka Lawson
Interior design and composition by Greg Johnson, Textbook Perfect

This is a work of nonfiction. All people, locations, events, and situations are portrayed to the best of the author's memory.

Post Hill Press
New York • Nashville
posthillpress.com

Published in the United States of America

CONTENTS

PART ONE

LIFE-CHANGING MOMENT

CHAPTER 1

The Backstory

You are about to read my story, my secret to success. This topic has graced countless articles, books (mine included), films, podcasts, and discussions: *Why is it that some people achieve success and others do not?* Some people are blessed to find it over and over throughout their life, while others are left chasing success forever. In reality, successful people are more alike than different.

I was instantly successful at a very young age. Being drafted in 2003 by the Jacksonville Jaguars at age twenty-two, I had a three-year contract for $1 million and an $80,000 signing bonus. That was my first "I made it" moment. For the normal person, that is a lot of money. However, in the National Football League, it wasn't. Money flies fast in the league. I played with guys who had huge contracts and signing bonuses, were dripping in diamonds, had multiple houses and cars. Yet even with all that, they would need a loan before the season even started to maintain their lifestyles. The problem was, situations like that were somewhat normal, and so no one ever acted as if they were in a financial predicament. Luckily for me, my brother and my dad were both in my ear about saving my money and not letting the money I now had get into my head. The NFL contracts are not guaranteed, and though I was young and had several years ahead of me, I always knew things could change fast. I did not want to be a statistic, as according to a *Sports Illustrated* article in 2009, more than 70 percent of NFL players are broke or bankrupt within two years of retirement.

I played on the offensive line. Many offensive linemen are almost awkwardly large. I was six-foot-six and 375 pounds and had very "normal" offensive linemen characteristics. We would kind of stick together. Our coaches and staff were always feeding us; keeping our size was important. I remember after every team break, coaches would urge us to go "get our snack in the conference room," which had tables and tables of sub sandwiches, chips, cookies, wings, pies...you name it, and this was our "snack." O-linemen don't talk much; we're the quiet type, but aggressive if provoked. The defensive line and running backs are typically the noise and flash on the teams. They like to be seen and heard, looking for media, buying the new designer clothes, and only driving the latest cars. These were the guys that were often looking to outdo each other on and off the field. If someone on the D-line gets a new car, the following week, there will be someone else with new rims or features on theirs to show. I didn't fit in with that group. I was just trying to stay healthy and play ball.

I owned one car throughout my whole NFL career, bought a house, and pretty much played video games and watched movies in my spare time.

Midway through my NFL career, my father's health issues increased, and he passed away. He was that person in my life that was my safety valve. In reality, he, along with my grandparents, were the only people in my life that I knew I had unconditional love from. I was twenty-five, and still needed my father's guidance. I was a mess. I didn't know what to do with my life. My dad had been to all of my football games since I was in high school. I always knew, regardless of the outcome, I had someone in the stands that really was there for me, and now I didn't. I know it may sound silly, but we were a football family. My dad played in college, my brother played in college and the NFL for twelve years, and now I did. This was "our thing," and now the thought of playing knowing my dad was no longer here was something I struggled with. It wasn't fun anymore. Shortly before I turned twenty-eight, I got an injury with the Tennessee Titans and decided to leave the NFL. Looking back, I wish I would have stayed and played a couple more years, but my heart was no longer in it.

When I left the NFL, I had between $500,000–$1 million in assets. I was young, and in reality, I was "fresh chum," the food you put in the water to attract the sharks. I see it happen all the time, but one of the scariest things is to watch young professional athletes leave the bubble of the sports world and become available for attack from people wanting to manipulate or get their hands on quick cash. The NFL does a pretty good job of protecting players from outside influencers as much as it can. When I was playing, I never had people approach me with business ideas. I was always geared toward just focusing on the game, but now everything had changed. I didn't have my dad for guidance anymore. My brother was trying to help me navigate my way, but he was still playing and had a family of his own. I was new on the scene, with investment cash, so many people were starting to show interest. However, before my dad passed away, he encouraged me to take a construction development class in the offseason. He was always trying to get me ready for life when the NFL was no longer an option. He thought I would be good in the construction world and could make an honest living outside of the NFL.

I started my construction company in 2007 in Baltimore, Maryland. Having no business experience, I sought to partner with people who had been in the construction world and knew how it worked (fresh chum, remember?). I knew I wasn't afraid to get dirty and be hands-on, and I was good at sales, but I couldn't also be a Chief Operating Officer or Chief Financial Officer. In the beginning, I was trying to find my niche between residential and commercial jobs. We did concrete and demo jobs mainly; we were small-time, but it gave me the time to get the hang of the construction scene. At this time, our biggest job had been about $500,000. We were steady and fine, but my partner and my staff encouraged me to start thinking bigger. They kind of helped to create an ego for me, and I jumped in. They convinced me to really be all in; I needed to invest my NFL money. That didn't really sit well with me, but again, they played to my ego and treated me like I was king. Over time, I became conceited and a bit more than arrogant about our abilities.

During this time, one of the largest minority contractors went out of business, which opened the door for my company to become the largest minority-run construction company and would thrust us in the big leagues with major general contractors throughout Maryland. We became a full dirt-work company and were now getting million-dollar projects on a regular basis. We were at the top. I was a young man with an eight-figure empire and an ego to match. We were doing it big. When I played in the NFL, I was always "Jonathan's little brother," or I was outshined by the noisier D-line, but now I would go around Baltimore and doors would be open, tables would be saved for me and my friends. I was living big at thirty years old with a very successful company. While this was fun, I wasn't the only one whose ego had gotten a little too large.

My partners and staff started feeling a bit entitled. Where regular companies maybe throw a Christmas party or give a small bonus at the end of the year, I was expected to take my staff and their families on an all-expense cruise trip—and the crazy part is, I did. Entitlement was as normal as a Monday morning football meeting. Things got out of hand fast. We were growing and doing well but were also gaining a reputation in the field that was less than stellar. We were winning jobs but my field guys were lazy, showing up to job sites drunk, and overall less than professional and costing me hundreds of thousands of dollars. I let the wrong people in my life influence me, and I put the wrong people in positions of power within my company. I remember at one point my brother telling me how he didn't trust my partner and I shouldn't do what he says, but I had a lot of people depending on me. I couldn't just walk away.

This spiraled out of control, and by 2013, I lost everything. I had to close my company's doors and file for bankruptcy for not only my business, but myself as well. A former NFL athlete who knew better than to spend his money too wastefully on things ended up losing it all anyway. I hated that I was a statistic. I was embarrassed and ashamed of my behavior. People were mad at me. My family was disappointed in me, my employees were angry, mainly because their money train and free trips were gone, but no one was more upset than me. My ego subsided and I was hit with reality.

I found myself with less than $1,500 in my account. How did this happen? I had nothing to show for my successes. I was just like those guys that I saw in the locker room that were so blinded by the fun they had to take loans to get to the next spot, except I had nothing to show for it. The banks made it very clear that I could no longer get loans. Here I was, ten years after I got drafted, and broke. The reality was, I wasn't completely alone anymore, though. If it were just me, I would have probably retreated to my brother's house in Vegas, played a ridiculous amount of poker, and figured something out. But I had a fiancée and a soon-to-be stepdaughter. I felt like a tool.

Many of my "friends" suddenly disappeared, as well as many family members. I never really gave myself time to grieve my dad's passing, and now here I was with nothing but time. I found myself being extremely self-deprecating, reliving all the horrible things people were publicly saying about me. Even though there were several factors that played into the fall of the business, and multiple partners, I was the face. I was the one that was supposed to save it. If there was ever a time I needed to pick up the phone and call my dad, it was now.

I left Baltimore and moved to North Carolina for a fresh start, but I really had no idea how to even create that. I couldn't sleep, I couldn't eat, but I still managed to find a way to drink a six-pack of beer every day. Soon, things went from bad to worse when the cars were repossessed. My fiancée bought me a truck for $1,800 from a local construction owner. I went to him to see if he had any available work, and I couldn't even get a job, but he didn't mind selling me an old work truck that was on its last leg. This was real...this was my life. The truck was rough, the "Green Machine," as we called it, but I was grateful. It had no heat, one radio station—a country station—and the passenger seat was barely intact. My fiancée wouldn't even ride in the truck, but it was enough for me. I definitely learned to love some Luke Bryan and Florida Georgia Line songs during that time.

I hated being so dependent on my fiancée. Not that she was set up financially—she had left her job as a teacher to move to Baltimore to be with me, so she had to find a job fast as well. We were definitely in a panic situation. I felt as though I wasn't the man she thought she was getting. I had let so many people down; I was so afraid to let her down as well. I wanted so badly to do something great. She was anxious that I would spiral and fall into a deep depression. She was right to feel that way, in all honesty. If I didn't have her in my life, it would have been easy to just give up, but I wanted so badly to make the one person who didn't walk away from me proud of me. I sat on my couch thinking for hours about what I could do to make money. I wasn't afraid to work, and my pride was gone, so I was open to anything. I wanted to tell my fiancée something good when she came home from work, to tell her I made money to help.

I went back to what I knew...football. I put an ad on LivingSocial to do a football camp with kids, not knowing what to expect. I was beyond shocked that within hours several people had bought the coupon. I cold-called the people who purchased the LivingSocial deals, and I sold packages doing one-on-one football trainings in my backyard. Within hours, I was outside creating drills with local Pop Warner athletes. In some way, getting back to football techniques was a sort of stress relief. It was familiar. I met some great families. They didn't know me from Baltimore, but they probably saw my truck and knew I had fallen on some difficult times. The mother of one of my athletes had a cleaning service company. She casually mentioned she was looking for someone to clean some of her company's business accounts on the graveyard shift. I was desperate for money at the time and would do anything to try to get ahead and lessen the financial load on my fiancée, so I offered to help. I took a part-time job with her company as a graveyard shift janitor cleaning office buildings for $8.25 an hour. I buried my pride and welcomed the extra income. I filled my nights listening to audiobooks or music, trying to pass the time as I cleaned cubicle after cubicle, break room after break room in downtown Raleigh. It was about five months later that I had my moment.

I feel like everyone at some point in their life has their "moment," the moment where they really decide what their life will be like. I definitely know that almost every successful person has had this moment, the moment of truth. The "What are you doing with your life?" moment, the "Wake the hell up!" moment, the "Are you freaking kidding me?" moment. I was halfway through my shift, listening to "Changes" by Tupac, emptying a break room trash can into the outside dumpster, when the bag broke and sour milk spilled all over my hands as debris spewed across the concrete. I shook the milk from my hands as the rotten smell drifted into the air. This was my moment...the spoiled milk moment. I sat on the curb and cried. I cried not because I think being a janitor is beneath me in any way, but because I knew this wasn't my story. I sat there and asked my dad what I was supposed to do, over and over. I needed guidance. I needed a mentor, someone to take me under his or her wings and say, *"Do this and you will be alright."* I knew I couldn't do this job, and if I stayed, I would get sucked in the trap of living someone else's dream, not my own. When I was finished speaking all my thoughts out loud, into existence, I sat and thought of the various people who came out of a struggle to find success and even peace. I thought of those people I would fill my mind with in my audiobooks and how so many of the successful ones had moments of pain. I kept being brought back to Tony Robbins, as he was also once a janitor and was now a multimillionaire keynote speaker, entrepreneur, and business coach. The point he stressed over and over was that *everyone* has a story. *I had a story.*

I know people look at me and the life I lived in the NFL and don't relate, but I was truly just like any other person. I dealt with loss, death, abandonment, being taken advantage of, making poor decisions, and needing a loved one to tell me it would be OK. I knew at that moment that I wanted to become a speaker and share my story.

CHAPTER 2

The Beginning

I wish I could say that it has been easy and that I became an instant success since then, but in reality, it was extremely difficult. I knew that I wanted to be a successful keynote speaker, and I scoured the internet and bookstores to follow leaders in the speaking industry. But I also knew I wasn't going to jump from being a night-shift janitor to a Tony Robbins overnight. I had no idea who I was, who my audience was, what my story would be, or if I was even relatable to people. I was also quite ashamed of my story. I walked away from the NFL after an injury because I was still so overwhelmed with grief. I had seen several articles or comments about my business failures online and struggled with the idea to share my fall from the top. I was embarrassed.

I called the NFL Player Care Foundation. I trusted them. In some way, I'm sure they felt that I utilized them as my own personal counselor at times, but they were always there and eager to lend an ear. I told them what I wanted and that I didn't know where to begin. They listened to me pour my heart out and encouraged me to share who I was outside of football. Don't relive the hype, don't be the Al Bundy of football, constantly reliving the highlight reel. I was always going to be a former NFL player. That's a title I earned. I was in the brotherhood. But the PCF reinforced that there was so much more for me to find out about myself, to make connections to other people with, and so much more time to evolve into a better version of myself.

The reality is that so many former players have no idea who they are outside of football. They give everything to the game, and when it's done, they feel like they have been forced out of the members-only club and don't know what to do with themselves. I'm sure if you think hard, you can name a few past players you know that only share former photos and videos or stories of the NFL on social media. I have seen it firsthand, guys that have several thousand followers on Instagram and are either popping bottles or sitting front row at games, yet will call their friends a week later to borrow one hundred dollars. Or you have guys that maybe never even made it out of training camp, but their titles are "NFL Athlete" and all their photos are of that one week in camp ten years ago. I knew I didn't want to be like that. I didn't want to just highlight the NFL in my life, but wanted to be authentic and real, to share the not-so-glamorous side of my story as well, and to find ways that I could relate to my audience.

After speaking to the PCF, I decided that instead of being the statistic that I knew the internet was going to make me out to be—the former player who lost all his money and ended up broke—I would talk about it. I would share the ups and downs, the egos, and the importance of having the right people in your life. I also welcomed this as a chance to heal from the wreckage. I needed to own it. My first job I booked was in December 2013. A guy I played basketball with in the mornings at the gym invited me to the Boys and Girls Club to speak to the kids. This was, of course, a non-paid event, as all my events were for over two years. But I was happy to have the opportunity to start somewhere, to practice the craft and get some experience. I thought kids would be easy to talk to. I'll play a little basketball with them and we'll be cool. Wrong! Kids are hard to speak to. Many times they don't have that social cue to laugh or help carry conversation. If I didn't have a football in my hand, they didn't care who I was. However, this was my audience. So here I go...

I went in there and totally overshared my problems. I don't think I taught them anything, as it was more of a venting session. I was a mess. Besides rambling and being incoherent, I wasn't organized, but I had passion. That passion was enough for me to want to do it again. I wanted to get better. I went to the director and my colleague who brought me in and was eager to get feedback. They were too nice, telling me I was great and would surely get better with time. I was excited. I had my first speaking opportunity under my belt and was ready for whatever was next. I went on to speak the next couple of months at a few local events, county meetings, and church groups, sharing my story with anyone who would listen.

During this time I was still training athletes at my house. There were these two brothers that were very diligent and trained hard in the offseason. Their father would often come, and I knew he worked for a respectable corporate company as the head of health care for the State of North Carolina. I eagerly told him my new profession and asked if he would pass along my name for any potential events. He agreed and called me a couple of months later, asking me to come to an event for his company. I would be the keynote speaker for the CXO dinner for NetApp in Chicago. I had no idea what NetApp did or that they were a Fortune 500 company. He told me they would take care of travel and lodging but would not pay me because I was a beginner. I was grateful to get experience on a corporate level.

I boarded my flight, feeling like a real keynote speaker. I was going to speak for a major corporate audience. I got to the hotel. It was very luxurious, and I felt like I had the red carpet rolled out for me. I got ready for the dinner. My driver picked me up. I loved the attention and was thinking that I had finally made it into the public speaking world. I went to the event and was full of passion. I knew I did my speech well and felt like I knocked it out of the park when I got a standing ovation at the end. I was excited about my new role and knew from this experience that I would start having corporate offers left and right.

A couple of days later, I got a call from my associate who recommended me for the job. He asked to take me to lunch. I thought he was going to tell me how great I did and was probably trying to book me for another job. He said, "Marques, you have great energy and passion, but you didn't stay on topic, and you didn't know your audience. You told your story and spoke about your failed business ventures, but we are a health care provider. We wanted to hear about CTE, concussions, football life, and injuries."

I'm sure my mouth dropped as it all clicked in my head. As my audience changed, my stories had to change, my deliveries had to change, and I had to be open to feedback to improve.

I'm sure you may be confused..."Wait, Marques, the PCF told you not to just talk about football and to be open about your other aspects, but then your first corporate job wanted to hear about football." The thing is, it was all a part of my story. I am a former NFL athlete. If that is relevant to what the client needs, then that's what I'll talk about, but there are other aspects as well—leadership, diversity, struggles, triumphs, health care, the corporate world, perseverance, grief, depression, addiction...these are all parts of my story that I have spoken on over the years and are found throughout my life. I spent time for the first six months really identifying who I was, who my audiences could be, and how I could be relatable to the various groups I spoke to. The underlying message is that, regardless if you are a speaker to a general audience or in the corporate world, you have to adapt to what your client needs to hear. You have various aspects of your story and who you are that can be fit to what your client needs and can relate to.

I called my buddy at the Boys and Girls Club, asking to come back. He graciously accepted, and this time I talked about my experiences as a child growing up in a single-parent household and going to the Boys and Girls Club every day after school. I talked about the resources I had there and how in turn many lessons I learned while playing ball after school at the Boys and Girls Club were lessons I took with me into my NFL career. I found ways to identify with those kids and had everyone's attention in the room, with rave reviews from my peers.

I am happy to say NetApp asked me back the following year, and this time I not only did my research on the company and their endeavors before going, but I also talked to them about their needs beforehand and made connections in a way they were privy to, leaving with several reviews flooding my inbox of how my story (the one they identified with) was powerful and insightful. This was one aspect of my speaking career that I had learned. It took time to learn and practice it, but I knew it would help to assist my call to action in my career.

PART TWO

HOW TO ACHIEVE SUCCESS

CHAPTER 3

Call to Action

I was still far from the ultimate success, but was having small victories during this time. I realized when I was initially trying to brand myself as a speaker that I had to do five things: number one, I had to promote myself. I didn't have money for a marketing team nor did I even know where to start. I wasn't afraid to work hard so I knew that meant that I had to tell people, everyone I came in contact with, about myself as a speaker. I knew my strengths. I was a people person; I could work a room and connect well with people. I had a good work ethic; I am still often the first one to events and the last to leave. I knew this about myself, so I knew that if I could get the chance to evolve as a speaker and focus on what I do well, I would eventually become successful. I told my friends and family my strengths as I promoted myself to my inner circle, asked for favors, and really shared my goals with people.

I know that I've lost some of you right there, that you are afraid of rejection and putting yourself out there. All I can say is get used to it, because I have yet to meet any successful entrepreneur that didn't face a mountain of rejection. In business in general, you have to develop thick skin in regard to rejection. Mel Robbins describes it as the "Avalanche Theory." This is when it feels like everyone around you—friends, associates, colleagues, family—will tell you your goal is not a good idea, and that you can't achieve it, and they discourage you from pursuing it. This will happen. Instead of running from it, identify it. The problem is that many people will start to share their goals and promote themselves, but when hit with a few bouts of rejection, they give up. I can't tell you how many times I heard, "Stick to football," "You should coach somewhere instead of being a speaker," or "No one is going to hire you." It's frustrating, I get it, but it's part of the experience. If you have a few people that give you a chance out of the many who reject you, you are still on your way to building your brand.

Looking back on my own development as a speaker, that job at NetApp was huge for me. I got the contact from promoting to my inner circle, and while so many other people in my circle laughed at me and mocked me, I had this significant colleague who didn't. And though it didn't pay, it was vital for me to evolve as a polished speaker. It doesn't matter if you are in the speaking industry or any type of entrepreneur, you have to promote yourself or your product to your inner circle. Stick with it, don't get discouraged, and you will eventually see those in that circle that didn't initially believe in you will see your value over time.

The second thing I had to do was to figure out what three main things I would talk about as a speaker. Initially, I chose to focus on leadership, transition, and perseverance. I needed to be broad enough to reach a variety of people, but also stay in my wheelhouse of experience. I was a leader, whether in football or in the business world when my company was at the top. I led my company to many top spots in Baltimore. However, I could also talk about the failed leadership skills I had, what not to do, and what I learned. I was arrogant, and that is not a good trait for a leader. I didn't vet people, and I hired people who needed help instead of people who were truly qualified for the job.

I could talk about transition. I know some of you reading this won't quite understand, but transitioning from the NFL to the regular world can be very difficult. I talk to my NFL brotherhood all the time about the transitions. You find that you are working your entire life to achieve the highest professional level of a sport, you achieve it and are on top of the world, but when it's over, it's over. The NFL absolutely spoils you. Besides making a pretty great salary, you get used to your game clothes being laid out for you, food ready for you all the time in the state-of-the-art cafeterias, on hand trainers, doctors, massages...anything you or your family needs is pretty much taken care of. It's a great privilege and honor to play in the National Football League. So, when you suddenly drive up to the gate and your key card no longer works (that is how some players would find out they were cut, including myself), that can be a shocking experience to try and transition from. You were once someone who the security guards would joke around with, you knew the staff on a personal basis, and now no one answers your call or acknowledges you. The other thing many athletes realize is, once they leave the NFL, they are not mentally prepared to do anything else with their lives. A significant number of former players have no work experience and are now entering the entry-level corporate career field. Many struggle with their pride.

Several guys I played with transitioned from financially taking care of multiple members of their families to not being able to anymore, but still being expected to. Besides the financial changes are the emotional changes. I dealt with this for some time. In the NFL, you are expected to be rough and filled with raging testosterone. It's not uncommon for guys to get into fights or scuffles on and off the field. The trash talking during a game is unlike anything I've ever heard. During a game, this seems normal, in a way; however, in the real world, this sort of behavior is seen as extremely hostile. Many guys have a hard time adjusting from the way they have been conditioned to be while playing to the normal everyday life away from the gridiron. I work with the NFL's The Trust and the NFL Retired Players Association to better prepare current and former players with their transition. However, I have found so many similar stories from so many people who are transitioning out of the military to a whole new career field. Transition can be difficult on everyone, and being able to help people in any way, sometimes just by acknowledging the struggle, is something I knew I was equipped to talk about.

Lastly, I focused on speaking about perseverance. From getting drafted to the NFL, to opening a business, to rebranding myself in a whole new field as a keynote speaker, I learned that perseverance is necessary for success. It's something many of us can relate to and find needed at various times throughout our careers.

The third thing I needed to do was to find clients. This seems simple, but can definitely be challenging. I had several clients who were willing to give me opportunities to speak for free. I went two-and-a-half years speaking for free before I got my first paid speaking job. I have so many people I coach now that want to become speakers and want to make $2,500, $5,000, $10,000 within their first couple months. It doesn't often happen like that, if at all. You have to get clients first, oftentimes for free or for very reduced prices. I was happy to have someone pay for my travel and accommodations in return for a review if they liked my presentation. As I said earlier, I knew my strengths. I knew I could work a room and possibly get leads for other jobs. I have had countless paying jobs that came my way through events I did for free. Doing events for free in the beginning allowed me to perfect my craft as a storyteller and keynote speaker. It helped me learn what worked and what didn't work in front of a crowd. I learned that I had to be adaptable. My clients and audiences changed constantly. I had to learn to ask my clients, "What do you want me to talk about?" What is their theme, what do they want me to stress to their audience? If I had slides, I would often send my clients a copy of my slides weeks in advance so they had an idea of how things would go. This level of professionalism and preparation is extremely important with paid clients; they need to be prepared as well. By doing this with my unpaid clients, it set the tone for me to keep it a practice regardless.

Another thing I had to make sure to do to gain new clients and retain others was look the part. When I first started speaking, I had earrings in both ears, would sometimes wear a button up shirt or T-shirt with jeans, and thought I looked like a speaker. I quickly learned that I had to completely revamp my look. If I wanted to be taken more seriously, I had to look like a keynote speaker in the realm I was in. I started wearing suits to my events; I became more polished and professional. There have been a few times when the client has asked me to dress in a more casual way for their audience, but all this is discussed ahead of time. Make yourself available, know your clients and audience, and use your strengths to retain a job.

A fourth thing I always did, and continue to do, is to ask clients to give me a testimonial. If my client mentions they liked my keynote speech, I absolutely will ask for a review. These reviews are vital for continued work. I tell my coaching clients to always ask for reviews. It doesn't matter if you are in the speaking world or have a product you are selling. When people buy from you, ask for a review; this is an absolute steppingstone to building your brand. I tell people all the time,

"What you say about yourself will build your self-confidence; what others say about you is *vital* to obtain new business and build your brand!"

The fifth thing that was needed when I started out and continues even today is a website. My first website was a conglomeration of football training and speaking services. People were confused as to what I was marketing or wanted. Was I a speaker or a football coach? If you have separate businesses that don't complement each other, you should have separate websites. I had to learn not to put all my NFL pictures on my website that promoted me as a speaker. The two careers had nothing to do with each other. Your marketing and promotional material needs to be clear and not limiting so people know what services you provide. Always make sure your reviews are on your website, and include clips of yourself at events. Most paying clients would never hire me unless they saw me speaking at other events, whether they were there or saw me on video.

Other things I did in the beginning of my career that continually have helped me throughout were setting benchmarks and planting seeds. Create a goal and work toward it. I was and am still always networking, going to events, talking to people, and really listening to what they want. If you are trying to build any successful business you have to *market, market, market*! I knew I was adaptable. I knew my strengths and what topics I had ready to discuss. I had a website with reviews to back up what I was marketing. Constantly evaluating and revamping your product is so important when branding yourself, whether you are looking to become a speaker or any type of entrepreneur. I found by completing these five steps, I was setting myself up for the Success Cycle to follow.

CHAPTER 4

Follow the Cycle

So here I was: I had an idea. I had a website and was sharing my new business venture with anyone and everyone. I should have been instantly successful, right? No. In my experience with business or dealing with other people starting a business, you have to give yourself time—time to fail, time to learn, and time to figure it all out. Most businesses take at least three to five years before they become successful because there are several factors and steps to achieve small successes before the big ones come.

Early on, I remember calling someone that worked for an NFL team. I had been associated with him before and I wanted to share my ideas with him and see if he would book me to talk to his new rookie class. I knew I could help these guys with my story in some way. I was excited to get on the call and be a part of something big we could do together. About five minutes into me sharing all my ideas, the guy on the other end cut me off and said, "Marques...I'm just taking this call as a favor to J.O. (my brother, Jonathan). Why would I hire you for this? You aren't the brother people want to talk to."

I was really quite stunned when I heard that said to me over the phone. It was rejection served on fine china. I was standing in my kitchen, wanting to return with a few choice words and hang up on his ass, but I took a deep breath and thanked him for his time and hung up. I was so defeated when I got off the phone. I was used to rejection, but this felt personal.

My wife was in the living room and I went and told her what had happened. It was so hard for me to shake. She sat there, listened, and threatened to call him back herself a few times, but reassured me I would be successful, not because of anyone doing someone else a favor, but because I was ambitious, driven, and hardworking.

She explained that I really had no other choice but to be successful with those three qualities. People who are ambitious never stop wanting more or to better themselves. They are typically driven to achieve those things and don't mind putting in the hard work to reach their goal. Later that night, while lying in bed, I thought of what she mentioned. I had no choice but to be successful. I just needed the right direction. I thought a lot of my brother, my father, and my childhood.

My parents divorced when I was eight years old. At that time, my brother was in high school and focused on football.

The Success Cycle

He was already being recruited heavily and it was clear he was going to go on and become a professional athlete. It was an exciting time, but it was also a sad time. I remember my dad working. He worked near Capitol Hill in Washington, D.C., in finance and was very successful. When I was early in my teen years, he fell ill with kidney failure and was unable to work. My brother went to college and was focused on his school and sports, rightfully so, and often times it was just me and my dad at home. There was a big financial strain. I didn't see it in its severity as a young teen but as an adult looking back, it was shocking. There were times that we had no food.

Now I know, by looking at me, I was a husky kid, so no one dared to think I was missing any meals. I was resourceful. I would go to my grandparents' house for dinner and visit my godparents for a second dinner. I didn't always know when I would eat again so I would take any opportunity I had. I know my dad was embarrassed about that.

Oftentimes we didn't have heat in the winter. We would light the stove and layer up. However, I never felt uncared for or unloved in any way. It was quite the opposite. My dad was amazing and loved big, but he lost his ambition and his drive because he was unable to work. He gave up, and as a result, we went without things we needed often. As he did that, I gained ambition. I wanted to take care of him and to create a life for us that would comfort him in his ailments. As I went through high school my goal was to play football in college; then in college, I wanted to follow my brother's footsteps and get into the National Football League. I had big goals. I was also naturally, without being prompted, extremely driven to make them happen. I missed out on a lot with friends because I was watching film or practicing, getting more reps in the weight room or just intentionally trying to stay out of trouble. I would often show up to workouts early and stay late. When I made it to the pros, I never stopped working hard. I was able, along with my brother, to take care of my dad in his final days in a way that I had wanted and intended to do since I was a child.

After the NFL, when starting my company, I knew I wanted to be something big outside of football. I knew I wanted something I could be proud of, and be a part of the city of Baltimore. I had huge ambitions when I partnered and took on various projects in the construction industry. I wanted to succeed while attending the various meetings with developers, providing quality craft and working hard to ensure both my team and clients were happy. Even though I made big mistakes where I learned about what not to do in business, I was a success with my construction company at one time as well.

As I lay in bed, I realized my wife was right; ambition, drive, and hard work have always been in the equation when success was achieved in my life. However, I never knew. I never gave thought to my actions in those terms. So, I dove deeper. What did it mean to have ambition? What did drive look like? And how did I work hard? Here I was starting yet again, and I had to identify my ambitions, develop my drive, and accompany it with hard work. However, this time, with those three key components in the forefront, I asked myself another question: What did I want? Did I want to be successful enough to feed my family and live a nice quiet life in Cary, North Carolina? Did I want to become the next Tony Robbins? It didn't matter what I wanted to achieve in my life, all I knew for certain was I had to start with the Cycle. Whatever lane I wanted to end up in, I needed to let my ambitions set the tone. So I created a goal right then. I drove to the twenty-four-hour drug store and got a few poster boards. I came home and wrote out my goals and my ambitions for the next five years on one poster board. On another poster board, I wrote my goals for the next twelve months, and on a third, I wrote my daily goals.

Then, on each one, I wrote, "Drive." What were characteristics of a driven person to reach those goals? What was going to make me continue on when I was tired? I wrote things like, "Get up an hour earlier to focus on my goals for the day," "Keep my commitments," "Prioritize my time," "Be more persistent,"

"Know why I wanted to do what I was doing," "Keep my future in mind," "Challenge myself," "Stay focused," and "Keep my eyes clearly on my future and my goals." The only way I was going to succeed was to stay laser-focused, with my drive helping to push me forward at all cost.

I then followed with "Hard work" and identified how I intended to do that with things like practicing my craft, networking more often, calling a certain amount of people a day, emailing a certain amount of people, paying attention to detail, working nights and weekends, developing myself, creating a team, joining a speakers support group, and getting more videos of my speaking abilities on social media to help market myself.

Of course, this is just on paper, a visual...and things change and should always be revamped and reevaluated for what works and what doesn't. I hung those poster boards in my office and constantly erased and rewrote things, but my ambitious goals were always present, at the top, and in mind with everything I did.

I had developed a cycle...a Success Cycle. I knew this cycle had worked before in my life. I identified these characteristics in myself—first, when I was pursuing my goal to play in the NFL, then again when I was building my construction empire. I really wanted to succeed in my new venture of being a keynote speaker, and I had learned more than enough lessons from my previous experiences and failures. I was ready to really achieve success on my terms.

I followed this cycle for five years. I stuck to it, using my drive and hard work to achieve my goal...and what happened?

I started checking off goals as they were being achieved, on poster boards, my twelve-month and my five-year plan boards. When I would finish one goal, I would add another and start the cycle again. I started finding myself in the groove; I had something that finally worked. I became even more disciplined to stay on track with each new ambition. Within five years, I not only became a bestselling author, but I spoke for various Fortune 500, Fortune 100, and Fortune 50 companies, hosted sold-out academies for new speakers, and launched a coaching career to help others learn how to create their success. I did a complete one-eighty in terms of who I was then, and who I am now in the success realm, learning and growing along the way. I am still a visual person in every sense of the word. I have notebooks filled with my new goals, and ideas on where my successes will take me and who I will become along the way. I keep it simple, focusing on ambition, drive, and hard work.

I work very closely with some NFL teams, the NFL Retired Players Association, the Retired NFL Players Congress, and the NFL's The Trust on the transitions current and former players make once out of the league. In doing this, I was asked by one of my former teams, the Buffalo Bills, to come and talk to their rookies every year. I talk to their new athletes about using their time wisely and creating a successful life on and off the field—what that looks like—and regardless of their future endeavors, also letting them know that we are a brotherhood and my door is always open. I was shocked one day to see an email pop up in my inbox from the guy who took my phone call *to do my brother a favor* earlier in my career. He poured out his support and acknowledged my successes since we previously spoke. To be perfectly honest, I wasn't sure how I felt about that email at the time, but if he was humble enough to reach out, I was humble enough to accept his regards. However, I also acknowledged that the rejections early on in my journey, even the ones that felt all too personal, made me develop a deeper understanding of the Success Cycle and why it has been so useful in my life. If I hadn't talked to him and felt rejected from his words and disbelief in me, I might have not gotten a plan in strict order to achieve success. For that, I was thankful.

So, this is what I know: there is no secret to success, no magic key we can turn, but there is certainly a cycle we can follow. I know this because I did this, and continue to do so. I know I can also help you use the cycle in the correct way that will ensure your success in your branding and/or business, no matter what area of business you are trying to embark on. As we go through the next several chapters and identify what each cycle requires and entails, start finding ways to apply it to your daily life. Get your poster boards ready, and really start to utilize the different ways to create the success you want in your individual life, on your terms, no matter what the nonbelievers might say.

PART THREE

AMBITION

CHAPTER 5

Set the Goal

The first part of the cycle is all about a strong desire to achieve something, which is your ambition. It is vital to identify your ambition that creates your goals early on in your cycle, as it drives the other two factors. I found that implementing six steps helped me set my goals in a realistic manner and kept my ambition alive.

The first two steps go hand in hand. First, I had to identify specific goals. When I started this practice, I wanted to become a keynote speaker; that was my overall goal. That was a very broad goal, however, and to achieve it, I had to be specific. I knew that I would have to set several small goals in order to reach my larger overall goal. This is going to change often and that's fine.

The second step is to set a time to achieve these goals. It is extremely important that you set realistic goals in a realistic time frame. For example, when I started this practice, I had daily goals, a goal for my first year, and a goal for my fifth year. These goals were vastly different. My goal every day was to talk to someone new about my venture into becoming a keynote speaker. I talked to people I knew, but never people in the industry. I had to expand my network and create new networks and leads through a variety of people, from local clubs to global companies. Every day, I made it a point to go outside of my comfort zone and talk to someone about keynote speaking, whether it was marketing myself or listening to others talk about speakers that left an impact on them. I wanted to hear about it, learn from it, and collect some type of nugget to add to my own craft.

My one-year goal was to actually get paid as a keynote speaker. One year...I gave myself one year. Was this a reasonable amount of time? Possibly. Did I achieve it? No. I didn't get my first paid speaking job within my first year as a keynote speaker. To be honest, I didn't even get my first paid job my second year. I went thirty months before I got a paid job. I did close to forty keynote speeches within those thirty months, and not one time did I get paid. However, I did get to build my résumé, get reference letters, get film to add to my website, expand my network, and practice a lot. Even though I didn't achieve my goal, I never lost sight of it. I didn't quit, and two-and-a-half years after I started this journey, I finally landed a paid job as a keynote speaker. I did the commencement speech for Miller-Motte College in Wilmington, North Carolina, for $1,500. I was so excited that I didn't even negotiate for a different price. I was probably too scared they would take their offer away. I was ecstatic. Clearly, I had worked hard for this and was happy to be able to finally reach my goal. I knew this was the first step, and now I would be landing high paying jobs all the time, right? That definitely didn't happen. However, I was heading in the right direction.

Many times I talk to people who are so overly eager to get to the next step, they almost expect it to happen overnight, or within a couple months, or maybe even within a year, and they don't understand that the time that's put in to actually achieve the goal is part of the process. I have had various people come to me that want to be keynote speakers. They may say they know their worth and won't take less than $5,000 or $7,500 to start. These are typically the same people who are so confused as to why they don't get booked. These are unrealistic goals. It's so important for your goals to be realistic and to be willing to adjust them. My goal was to get a paid speaking job my first year; it didn't happen. My goal my second year was to get a paid speaking job, and I worked hard for it; it still didn't happen. But that third year, when it did, I was able to really deliver an experience for my client that was very practiced and poised from two years of practice. My goal was never to get paid a certain amount, just to get paid. It could have been one hundred dollars; I would have reached my goal. Keep it simple, keep it real.

If you are setting goals that are not realistic, you won't succeed. Focus every day on achieving the small goals that turn into bigger wins. The wins then build momentum and that momentum leads to bigger jobs and successes.

My five-year goal was to become a known speaker in the industry. I met that goal. Even though my path to my long-term goal didn't go as expected, I was still able to adjust and keep the energy in line with the overall intent.

The third step in setting a goal is that it must be written down. Regardless of whether you have daily, yearly, or long-term goals, they all must be written out. This is actually something many people do already, but it is very crucial for your success. Writing your goals is a way to bring them to life, to affirm them and make them important. Not only is writing down your goals, or even creating a vision board, a good practice for keeping your thoughts in line for what you are aiming toward, but it also does something neurologically at the same time. There is an encoding process that happens in our brain as to how decisions are made, as to what gets stored in our memory and what gets discarded. Writing improves that process, meaning that it has a greater chance of actually being remembered. This practice is commonly seen in education purposes for taking notes; it triggers your brain to remember the content.

I sat in a workshop once where Dr. Gail Matthews, a psychology professor in California, shared a recent study she participated in on the art and science of goal setting. She discussed how she gathered 267 people together—men and women from all over the world, and all walks of life, including entrepreneurs, educators, health care professionals, artists, lawyers, and bankers. She divided the participants into groups, according to who wrote down their goals and dreams, and who didn't, and she discovered that those who wrote down their goals and dreams on a regular basis achieved those desires at a significantly higher level than those who did not. In fact, she found that you become 42 percent more likely to achieve your goals and dreams simply by writing them down on a regular basis.

The fourth step is to develop a plan to achieve your goal. As I previously stated, I had a daily goal, a one-year goal, and a five-year goal. My daily goal was to talk to someone new about my brand as a keynote speaker. This wasn't difficult to do. I emailed new people, went to networking events, and even did cold calls at times. I was determined to expand my brand. My one-year goal was to get paid as a keynote speaker. This goal was more challenging, as it wasn't until my third year that I actually reached it. I had to develop a plan, then fail, then develop a *new* plan. This is the part where I see so many people quit. Sometimes the plans work, sometimes they don't. What happens when you feel you have a great plan and then you fail? What do you do? I often times think of where I would be today if I would have given up on my plan to become a keynote speaker after failing on my one-year goal. What about if I would have quit after still failing two years in?

The reality is, I didn't quit, but I *changed.* I absolutely had to reevaluate my plan to achieve the goal. What I was doing was not working. I was talking to the wrong people, not marketing myself enough, not accepting constructive criticism, not tailoring my keynote speeches to my audience, and so on. I get asked all the time by people, "How long do you give yourself before throwing your hands up and accepting that you need to move on?" Here's the thing...I don't move on, I change the plan. I knew I could be a good keynote speaker. I wanted more for my life than what everyone expected of me. This was my choice and I was going to make it work, but that required learning, failing, and learning again. I read Steve Harvey's book, *Act Like A Success, Think Like A Success*, during this time, and there was a sentence in the book from Warren Buffet which has stayed with me over the years. Mr. Buffet said he wouldn't do business with anyone who has not failed at least three times. Think about that—not just failed and learned, but failed, learned, failed more, learned more, and failed again. There is so much valuable insight that is found in failure that it is absolutely a part of success. It doesn't feel like it at the time, but in the long run, you will appreciate it.

Your plan has to change. Through that, you will find what works. Because my plan changed over and over again, I was able to achieve my five-year goal. Don't be discouraged; success doesn't come easy, which brings us to the fifth step.

You must decide the price you are willing to pay. What are you willing to sacrifice to achieve the goals you are setting? So many people I know are working full-time jobs while trying to create a new brand or entrepreneurship. I worked long hours. It wasn't a nine to five week; it was often a ninety-five-hour week. I have met so many people that I have watched walk away from new networks and potential deals because they were "off the clock." To put it bluntly, your job pays your bills, but your vision will make you rich. You have to come home, even after working a full-time job, and use those evening hours or the weekend to fuel your visions and goals. It won't happen fast, but over time, you will get to work less at a job and more and more on your own goals. This means sacrifice. This means your family will sacrifice, so it's imperative they have the same mindset. My wife understood the goal. It was her goal as well, and sometimes me going to a networking event or dinner with a potential client was time well spent for our family to succeed.

However, let me make it clear: during the two years I tried to get a paid speaking job, I never was without a paycheck. I always kept a regular job, whether that was training kids in football, running a flag football league, running summer camps, and so on. I never went without a job. I meet people all the time who tell me they are creating their new brand or company, or even want to do public speaking, but they refuse to have a regular job while they build their career. Unless you are financially funded, it doesn't work like that. Unfortunately, many people who have told me that find themselves in financially dire situations shortly thereafter. There will be many sacrifices you will make while creating your brand and finding success, and time will always be one of them.

The last step to reaching a goal is to actually think about your goal every day. If you are not obsessed with it, you will be average. My goals kept me awake at night, and woke me up in the mornings. They still do. I have been told I work too much. I have been told I'm too intense about work. However, my ambitions from "working too much," or "being too intense about work" have helped me reach all my goals and allowed me to not only create new ones to take me to the next level, but to also make my brand my full-time job. There's never a day off from thinking about my goals. I keep it fresh, in the center of my mind, evaluate what works and what doesn't, align myself with people that are on the same path or even remove myself from people who are not, learn from others, and help people along the way. Your goals will change. You will complete them and/ or make new ones. However, your approach to achieving them should remain the same.

1. Have a specific goal.
2. Create a time frame to achieve the goals (daily, one year, five years...).
3. Write down your goal.
4. Create a plan to achieve the goal.
5. Decide what price you will pay to reach your goal.
6. Think about your goal every day.

PRACTICE

Use this space to identify your goals:

Daily Goals

_____

_____

_____

_____

_____

_____

_____

_____

One-Year Goals

_____

_____

_____

_____

_____

_____

_____

_____

Five-Year Goals

_____

_____

_____

_____

_____

_____

_____

_____

CHAPTER 6

Stepping Out of Your Comfort Zone

As I mentioned in the last chapter, in order to be great at your goal, you have to be obsessed with it. You have to think about your goals and constantly be reevaluating what works and what doesn't work. Another huge part that plays into that is oftentimes stepping out of your comfort zone. That's where the magic happens.

In reality, we are all creatures of habit. Many of us wake up at the same time every day, eat the same breakfast every day, drive through the same coffee shop on the same route to work, go by the same grocery store on our way home, and so on. We like what's familiar. It's safe. It's comfortable.

As an entrepreneur, it's common to be faced with decisions to take risk, and that can be scary. When I first started my plan to become a keynote speaker, I had so many people tell me I had no business in that field and should stick to football. In some regards, they were completely right. I had no experience in the field and no real idea of how to achieve my goal. I also wasn't in a financial position to be able to fund myself if I failed. I had to step out of my comfort zone and learn about the new world I was entering. Eventually, what was once unknown and frightening became normal.

The only way to get most people out of their comfort zones and break habits is to actively change the way they are thinking.

There have been so many people before us that have created bountiful amounts of greatness from simply stepping outside their comfort zone and thinking outside the box.

- ▶ Fred Smith, the creator of FedEx, was given a C on a paper he wrote about his idea for getting packages to people overnight. He was laughed out of several meetings to raise capital, but continued his pursuit and changed his way of thinking to achieve it. And FedEx is now the world's largest transportation company, providing deliveries throughout hundreds of countries.

- ▶ Walt Disney was fired as a newspaper editor because he "lacked imagination." He went on to declare bankruptcy several times before thinking outside the box and creating Disneyland, which was originally rejected by the city of Anaheim. Worldwide, Disney brought in more than $45 billion in revenue last year.

▶ Dr. Seuss's first book was rejected by twenty-seven publishers until being picked up by the twenty-eighth and going on to sell millions of copies.

What these examples and countless others teach us is when one thing doesn't work, expand your realm and try again.

You have to stretch yourself, and it doesn't matter if it's in a small or big area. For example, you may believe that attending networking events weekly or monthly, sharing your story with people frequently, hiring a mentor or coach, or even asking people what you want would be something that's not in your realm to naturally do. However, small changes like those can make huge impacts overall in your business and brand. I think so many times we let the fear of rejection deter us from simply asking for what we want. The anticipation and fear of the negative response is enough to derail us and make us question our purposes. Approach it differently and almost expect the rejection. You will be rejected more than you are accepted. In certain areas of my profession, I still experience this, and it's OK because those few that accept you and want to work with you are the ones who you will create amazing things with.

I hear people tell me all the time that they feel pushy or demanding if they are expressing their desires. I respond by asking what their commitment is to achieving the goal? If this is something you really want and desire for yourself or your business, you will find the courage to push through.

However, it's important when simply asking for something that you are aware of what that might cost you. For example, if you ask for a raise, it might be granted, but might also come with more responsibility expected from you. Being aware of the potential outcomes is very important.

In addition, it's also necessary to ask without fear. I know this is easier said than done at times, but fear is just an emotion that blocks your capacity to receive. Sometimes people fear the rejection, but at other times, people fear the very thing they are asking for because of the associated responsibilities or the chance for failure. For example, I had a friend who was obese. He wanted desperately to lose weight, so he joined a gym, changed his eating habits, and even had surgery to remove excess weight. He successfully lost weight; however, over time, I saw him gain the weight back. He stopped going to the gym, started eating the same foods as before, and found himself in the same position. I asked him what happened, since he was so successful originally. He said he realized he was afraid to be thin. It was too much pressure for him to keep the weight off. As an obese person, he felt more comfortable. He was afraid of the responsibility associated with being thin, the accountability.

He went on to deal with his fear and got healthy again, but that fear of associated responsibility is a real thing that can show itself in your personal or professional life.

Finally, ask with trust. If you do not believe that you are worthy of receiving, then it will be completely obvious and you will get overlooked. No one wants to invest in or help someone who doesn't believe in themselves or their product.

Besides these ideas of being fully committed to what you are asking for, being aware of what comes along with what you are asking for, asking without fear of the outcome, and asking with the trust in yourself to achieve your goals, there are challenges that might arise when you step out of your comfort zone.

The first challenge that many people face when they step out of their comfort zone is being authentic. Many times, when people step out of their comfort zone, they feel fake. Maybe it feels unnatural for you to pitch your desires to a person or group of people, or to market in a way that doesn't seem normal to you. This is where doubt creeps in, and in reality, that's part of the process. We all feel doubtful when we are doing something we don't normally do; it is a normal step. You will live in this constant reevaluating mode for several years at the beginning. Sometimes people get too nervous about this and back off, but knowing ahead of time that the doubt is normal, and finding a happy medium where you feel authentic but still confident presenting your business, brand, or even self, is part of achieving the overall goal. I also encourage people during this time to accept the growth. We should always be evolving into a better version of ourselves, growing with the challenges. It feels unauthentic until you make it a part of who you are and your life. Embrace the change, as it is a natural part of the growth process.

Another common challenge people face stepping outside the box is feeling incompetent. I can personally relate to this. I had the desire to become a keynote speaker but I was no Tony Robbins or Les Brown. I had to acknowledge that and tailor my own personal strengths to become who I was supposed to be. In reality, if people wanted a Les Brown or Tony Robbins, they would find them; that role was already filled. I had to be a Marques Ogden and with that I had to have the confidence in myself to know that Marques Ogden was enough and was who other people wanted to hear from. Of course, that didn't mean I wouldn't learn from the people who successfully went before me, but my approach had to be different. Many people struggle with the acceptance factor in this challenge. You have the fear of doing something new and creating success, but now a whole new issue of acceptance rears its ugly head. I had been successful in the sports world. I was a vested NFL player with a pension and so forth, yet now I was struggling with feeling accepted and incompetent in this new field. Transmitting your success from one area in your life to another is not easy. Just because I successfully made a career for myself in the NFL and played for several years didn't mean that the rest of my ventures would be the same. This realization breeds the feeling of inadequacy. However, once you come to identify this feeling and come to terms with the realization that you are in control of your successes or failures, the wave of personal acceptance can wash over you. Letting go of the fear and just going for it can be one of the greatest feelings. This feeling makes the challenge completely valuable. This is why I love the *Rocky* series; it exemplifies the true meaning of letting go of your fears, and just going for it!

Resentment is a third challenge people feel when stepping out of their comfort zone. You may be an introvert and feel resentful that you have to go to networking events and work a crowd in order to become more successful. You may also resent having to step out of your comfort zone in general. I definitely struggled with resentment as I was out pushing my grind, doing everything I could possibly do, and watching other people be successful. I had to step out of my comfort zone and take accountability and find my areas of weakness to pay attention to. I was annoyed, frustrated, and resentful, but that doesn't help get the job accomplished.

Lastly, people are hesitant to step out of their comfort zone due to questioning their likability factor. This is a difficult one to measure. Being likable could mean different things to various people, and in most cases, all of us are likable at times and possibly jerks at other times. My wife and I always laugh because people always think she's mad. It's her expressions; she just doesn't think to smile or go out of her way to talk to strangers. I, on the other hand, am always talking to strangers, smiling and laughing. Being six-foot-six, I found people get a little intimidated by my size; however, I have been termed "likable" and my wife often jokes she must be "unlikable." However, she does point out she has more close friends than I do, so she's kind of likable.

The likability factor varies, and for some people, like me, it just comes naturally. I like to talk to people, smile, or wave. I'm a morning person, generally pretty chipper and excited about my day. Other people—like my wife, for example—have to be mindful of how they go about their day in regard to likability. This is obviously challenging to some and not as much to others. In the business world, likable people are genuine. They know what they do well and deliver it genuinely. They are credible. They say what they mean and mean what they say, and do what they say they are going to do. Likable people in the business world tend to do the right thing. I'm not talking about doing what will make people happy, but actually doing the right thing. This may correlate to why so many people have a disdain for politicians.

Likable people also tend to make good choices. Making good choices on a daily basis will lead to options and opportunities. In reality, the only true thing people have control over is the decisions they make and the actions they take. Instead of worrying about what other people think or feel, implement these ways to make yourself more likable, and it won't be so much of a challenge.

In reality, part of ambition and goal setting is to step out of your comfort zone, think outside the box, and really push yourself in various ways to achieve your goal. There's not one path that's right for any one person or any one business idea. It's absolutely imperative to expand your actions and thought process to meet the ultimate success. I have found that I might have several goals that I want to achieve, and I have to use different methods for each one to reach my targeted destination!

PRACTICE

Identify ways you can get out of your comfort zone.

1. _____

_____

2. _____

_____

3. _____

_____

4. _____

_____

CHAPTER 7

Creating Your Road Map to Success

A long with setting realistic goals and stepping outside of your comfort zone, in order to really achieve your goals with your ambition, you have to be able to create your personalized road map. Your road map is a timeline, an outline, and the steps needed to actually achieve the goal. I've heard it said many times, a goal without a plan is just a dream. I have met many dreamers. There are people who come to me all the time with dreams of this or that, but they have absolutely no plan on how to fully achieve it. Don't get me wrong, it's OK to dream. I'm honestly a dreamer naturally, but I've learned the dream goes nowhere if I don't plan for it. I knew a gentleman years ago that would always say, "I'll meet you at the top," or, "We're on our way to the top." I loved his positivity but he had absolutely no plan of action to get to the top, just the fortitude to announce he was going to be there one day. Years later, nothing has changed in his branding because there was no actual course of action. Being ambitious is one part of the Success Cycle, but laying out the steps to guide that ambition and following them will make your goal successful.

I know I mentioned it before, but every goal is different. The path is going to change to achieve each goal you set for your brand. You have to find the road that works for what you are trying to reach and achieve. For example, take a kid who is so excited to get their license. Their goal is to get their license when they turn sixteen. So, their personal road map would be making sure they have enough time to get into Driver's Education, take the written tests, take the driving tests, and have a year on the road with their learner's permit before they turn sixteen. These are the steps needed to achieve their intended success. However, what if they fail the vision test? Their road map has to change. They have to detour to go get their eyes checked and get a new prescription before continuing.

There will be things that pop up on the road map that you didn't consider, but more often than not, those things will help you be successful overall.

Years ago, I tried to start my one-on-one coaching business with clients. I was having success with speaking, and people would reach out to me and want to know how to get started in speaking or various leadership roles. I created a successful speaking academy with my wife. We hosted the academy twice a year for other leaders to come and learn the basics of how to start and create your brand, as well as network with companies looking to hire speakers. Many people would come up to me afterwards and want specific instructions on their personal goals, tailored to their specific needs. This created an opportunity for me to expand my brand. I decided I would start doing individual coaching with people to create the one-on-one training for their specific business needs and help connect people that I thought would work well together. I had a good idea, a good goal. It was realistic, but I had no road map of how to actually achieve it.

I work a lot with the NFL Retired Players Association and the NFL's The Trust. They had seen the success of my speaking academy and would often brainstorm new ideas with me for players transitioning out of the NFL into the next part of their life. During this time, I would often speak with Andre Collins, who is a good friend and the executive director of the Professional Athletes Foundation at the National Football League Players Association (NFLPA) about my different ideas. With assistance from The Trust and the NFLPA, I had managed to successfully transition and create a successful lifestyle. Andre became a sort of mentor to me, and I would often call him and bounce ideas off him. He knew I was struggling to get my coaching business off the ground, and he gave me a call and told me about an opportunity. The National Athletic and Professional Success Academy (NAPSA) was holding a professional development workshop, and Andre suggested I go. NAPSA's mission was, "Bridging athletic excellence to professional success." I didn't know what I was really attending, but I trusted Andre and knew I needed to step out of my comfort zone and create a plan, along with a road map, to achieve success in my executive coaching venture.

The event was the following week at Penn State in Pennsylvania. There were seven former NFL athletes selected to attend this five-day, intensive, hands-on program. We worked from eight in the morning to about six in the evening with a highly skilled team from NAPSA, which included the founder and CEO, along with all of their executive management team. Upon my arrival, I knew this was a rare experience, and I was eager to take advantage of every moment. The program was created to help each of us learn how to channel our abilities from the football field into business/corporate success. The NAPSA experience is designed to help reveal your hidden skills and knowledge and connect these competencies to the business world. It was a program to accelerate the transition to the next chapter of my professional life and was exactly what I needed. There were days of role play and scenarios, preparations, executive coaching, and personalized preparation for success. I met with each representative there to gain insight and knowledge into what my next steps should be for my one-on-one coaching business, and I developed a road map to achieve it. This professional development program specifically influenced me to learn how to authentically engage people and become more marketable in the corporate environment. I left with a detailed plan and how to execute it as well as a bigger network to interact with.

What I learned was, even though I was successful in other areas (speaking, creating a speaking academy, and the like), I was gaining no traction with my coaching career. The road map and lanes that I used for the others weren't working for this goal. I was at a dead end and had to detour, or pivot. This was a totally different goal and needed a different road map entirely. With assistance, I was able to map out my road map specifically for my coaching career. At that time, I had retained one client in six months. Six months after the NAPSA experience, I was working with over fifteen clients. Years later, still using the same road map that was created during that time, I have over thirty coaching clients. My original road map wasn't producing anything. I had to pivot, gain information and knowledge from other people, attend professional development conferences, step out of my comfort zone, and listen to experts on how to adjust, grow, and continue to develop in my craft. Some roads are wide and easy; there's plenty of room for error and space to move around. Other roads are narrow and may even end up at a dead end. You back up and try again.

You have to learn to reach out to your trusted inner circle and allow it to give you guidance in your life and business. In Andre, I had a mentor and friend who I trusted and was honest with. I told him about my idea to do one-on-one coaching and the various difficulties I had faced. I trusted his input and he led me to a program that was exactly what I needed to get my goal to the next level. Of course, I can sit here and endorse

NAPSA, as I obviously had a great experience in their program, but there are so many amazing professional development programs in our society. Whether you find yourself stuck in a situation where you can't get to the next level—or even identify what the next level is—reach out to mentors, get executive coaching, and use trusted programs to clearly identify your road map and the steps needed to achieve it. Know along the way there will be bumps and detours, but keep the goal in mind and follow the road map to achieve ultimate successes.

Though each road map may be different, there are three things that are important in each one. The first thing should be always keeping the targeted destination or goal in clear and concise focus. If you don't know where you are going, how will you know if you have been successful or not? Learning this after my failed construction company made me take a look at that business. We weren't long-term successful because I never had a targeted destination in mind. Even though I had massive success and grew the company, I was doing so without set goals to help drive me to my destination. I got derailed with the glitz, the money, and the ego; I didn't look at the big picture of where I was trying to take my company. You have to have the targeted destination in mind the entire time you are on the road map.

The second thing every road map should have is actionable steps to take to build small daily wins toward reaching your goals. In any business, continuing to network and talk to people to grow awareness around your brand and expand your inner circle is vital.

For me and my businesses, it's imperative that I grow my networking circle and inner circle constantly. When I was at NAPSA I learned that, as a coach, I had to be able to relate to my clients and understand their vision. I had to talk to people, find out who they are and where they were trying to go in order to relate to them. I took time for everyone. People buy from or hire who they like, so focus on being likable. I met a guy on LinkedIn a year ago. He emailed me, and I replied and got to know him, what he does, and what he is looking to do. He worked for a Fortune 200 company. I didn't ask him for a favor. I got to know him and created an authentic relationship with him. A few months later he reached out to me and wanted to introduce me to people in his network and said he felt I would be a great speaker for his company's big event at their corporate headquarters. I eagerly expanded my network and went on to be hired to speak for the company a few different times. If I would have never responded to him, or even responded only to ask him for a favor right away, I wouldn't have gotten the opportunity. Creating value for others without having an agenda really helped me expand my network. However, let me clarify—I know in previous chapters we discussed not being afraid to ask for favors or opportunities. I didn't meet him and initially ask for his network or his company to hire me. I got to know him, his values and beliefs, asked how I could be of service to him, and created a real rapport to gain a value-filled relationship and add him as part of my trusted inner circle. He would probably say I never shy from asking him for favors now that he is one of my best friends.

The third thing on every road map should be coaches or mentors. People that have expertise in the field you are trying to get involved with, to help you navigate the road correctly, should always be on your road map. Reach out to people who are good at what they do. Learn from people who have successfully achieved what you seek to achieve. Gain the knowledge, the expertise, and the resources. Brad Mitchell, CEO of NAPSA, who personally coached me, is absolutely why I began to have success as a coach myself. The way he was able to identify what I was or was not doing to enhance my success in that area was key to being able to move forward effectively as an executive coach.

Take a look at your road map below and identify your three steps. Write down your targeted destination, your actionable steps for achieving daily wins, and potential coaches or mentors that would benefit your road map.

1. _____

_____

2. _____

_____

3. _____

_____

PART FOUR

DRIVE

CHAPTER 8

What Is Your Why?

So, we have already established the first part of the cycle: ambition. We have set your realistic goals, found ways to step outside the box, and created a road map to achieve those goals. The second part is: drive. Your drive is what is going to make you continue to work even when you don't initially see results. Your drive will override your exhaustion when you hit a wall. Your drive will plow the frustrations of wanting to give up. We discussed that, on your road map, you will likely come to a dead end or have to detour. Your drive will keep you persistent and inspired in order to actually not give up, but continue to strive to meet those goals.

Creating a new business, brand, or entrepreneurial task is not easy. You are going to put so much time and energy into creating success, and you have to know the reason *why* you are doing what you do. What is your *why*? Some people refer to it as their mission statement, manifesto, or even purpose. What is the reason you are going to succeed regardless of anything life throws your way? Is it your family? The desire to provide a certain lifestyle for your family? To create security for your family for generations to come? Is it for financial freedom and the ability to set your own rules, or to travel more? Whatever the reason, it has to be strong enough to push you through the periods of struggle.

Expect it to be difficult. If you are starting a new business, do not expect things to be easy. You can make a timeline and a plan, and sometimes for reasons out of your control, you will have to adjust it. Your drive is what will make you not throw in the towel or walk away.

My parents divorced when I was very young. I grew up with my dad and my brother. As I mentioned earlier, my dad was a bank manager for the Federal Home Loan Bank of New York in the D.C. office. He was successful and took good care of us. In eighth grade, my brother was six-foot-nine and weighed 340 pounds. He was already being recruited to play football. He attended the top private school in the D.C. and Maryland area. He went to school with the Marriott grandchildren, the Rockefeller family, as well as Jesse Jackson's son. However, it wasn't cheap. My dad used his savings to put my brother through school.

It was a huge financial bill for my dad, but definitely promised some of the best coaching for my brother's natural talent to shine through. Toward the end of my brother's high school, my father's company was downsizing, and for whatever reason, my dad lost his job. Also during this time, he got diagnosed with kidney failure. This not only made it extremely difficult for him to find a new job, as he was in a health crisis, but it also made him a medical liability for companies and deterred his success in getting a new job. I was about twelve years old at the time and our quality of life went from having what we needed to being desolate. My brother was playing ball in college and it was just me at home.

Let me be clear when I say, I love my dad more than I can even explain, and in no way am I trying to broadcast or showcase his difficulties. However, as a man and father now myself, I can't imagine how he felt knowing there were times when he was unable to provide not only for himself, but also for his son. We didn't have basic necessities like heat, food, and sometimes, even water. He was proud and didn't want to ask for help, and I understand that. He didn't take care of his health either. He didn't have insurance and couldn't afford it, so his health continued to decline. When I was fifteen, my brother got drafted and came back to Baltimore. He realized what was happening and now had the resources to help. He paid for our house and household bills, bought my dad a car, and gave my dad spending money. In every sense, he took care of the both of us for the remainder of my high school years. However, during this time, my dad's health continued to decline, and he seemed to give up. As a man, it's common that your pride is wrapped up in how you provide for your family. It's almost linked to your ego or your natural identity. My dad could not provide for his family, and really even for himself. He never tried to find another job or revive his career. He never remarried, even though he had a relationship with someone who loved him dearly. I really think it was him, knowing he couldn't be who he wanted to be for her. He eventually gave up on his health and passed away when I was twenty-five years old, leaving me and my brother behind.

This is my *why*. I watched my dad struggle for years. I watched him lose a sense of himself when he couldn't be the father he intended to be. I watched him decline both financially and health-wise, mentally and physically. He gave up. I still needed my dad at twenty-five. I still need my dad today. Fast forward to today. I have two daughters. I don't want to leave my girls with that feeling. I don't want my girls to be cold or be without basic needs. I have to succeed. I have to stay sharp. I have to stay healthy and astute. I understand accidents happen, and I can't predict the future, but if I can give myself the best chance to fight my family health history to make sure my own family has what they need both now and in the future, I will. This is so extremely important and personal to me that it feeds my desire to succeed. My *why* keeps me focused on my goal, even when I'm tired or frustrated or feel like I've expended all options and am at the end of the rope. My dad was one of the best people I ever knew. People that knew him often tell me they see him in me as an adult. He had a huge heart and was generous. He was a fierce protector and so loving, but he gave up on himself, and in doing so, taught me one of the most valuable lessons: don't give up.

When I had my construction company, I did not have a *why*. I had a goal—be successful and make money—but it wasn't specific. There was no road map on how to achieve it. I worked hard and that was definitely what helped me achieve the goal, but it was never sustained because my drive was not supported by my *why* as well as other factors. I also didn't surround myself with or employ people with the same mindset, knowing their *why*. After brief success, it eventually failed. Hard work cannot carry the weight of the goal without the drive. The drive will never sustain the goal without a clear *why*.

When you are considering, really considering, why you are trying to be successful, or create something new, or start a whole new career, I encourage you to really search your reasons. The *why* is a key component of keeping that drive alive. It doesn't have to be as dramatic or telling as mine, but as long as it is real and creates a fire in you to do whatever you have to do to keep the goal afloat, that's your *why*. You may have more than one *why*. That's great; the more reasons you have to continue, the better. Your *why* may change with every undertaking and that's OK. Our lives change, and we change individually over time, so it makes perfect sense that your *why* might change. It is just absolutely imperative to your success that you know what it is. There will be times when you are physically, mentally, and emotionally exhausted on the road to success. We will talk more about that when we get to the last part, but it will happen. In reality, the *how*, and the strategies you implement, will become so much easier after you know *why*. Knowing this is what will get you through, help you readjust your plan or your team, and stay headed in the right direction. When you truly know your *why*, you will align your behavior with your goal and get your work done, day in and day out.

You may be reading this and not know your *why*. That's OK. Your *why* will always be simple and clear, accompanied with actions, and focused. This is when you start to ask yourself the following questions to determine what it looks like to you:

- ▶ What inspires you?
- ▶ What are your visions?
- ▶ How much money do you want to make?
- ▶ When do you want to retire?
- ▶ What kind of future do you want to create or provide for your children or family?
- ▶ How much vacation time do you want?
- ▶ Where do you want to visit?
- ▶ What do you want for your spouse or significant other?
- ▶ What does your ideal legacy look like?
- ▶ How do you want to make a difference in the world?
- ▶ What do you want to contribute to or be a part of outside of business?

Now that you have looked at your life and answered questions related to your life and how you want it to look, it is time to draft your *why* statement. This statement is a staple piece for your success. It should be at the top of your vision board and forefront in almost all decision-making toward achieving your goal. I was in a workshop years ago where there was a breakout session focused on establishing your mission statement. The format used was *"To ____ so that ____."* The first blank represents your action or contribution and the second is the result or impact.

For example, my *why* for this book is:

"To invest in and educate people so that they may achieve their goals and find success."

My actions are to invest or educate so the impact for others can be to achieve success.

Another example of my *why* for my speaking academy would be:

"To create an event and build an environment so that valuable learning and networking take place collectively."

My actions to create and build with the result of learning while networking was achieved at one setting.

Now it's your turn:

Grab a pen and take your time answering your statement. You may draft as many statements as you need to find the one that really identifies with your goal.

"To _____,

so that _____."

"To _____,

so that _____."

"To _____,

so that _____."

"To _____,

so that _____."

CHAPTER 9

What Is Your Vision?

We have already figured out your *why*. Now it's time to identify your vision. Your vision is the ultimate goal that steers your drive in the direction of success. Your vision is your long-term forecast for your brand or company. I know earlier in this book we talked about goals and how it is important to have daily goals, one-year goals, and long-term goals. However, your ultimate vision is going to be what those goals are chasing. One of the biggest mistakes a business owner can make is to think in the short term. Statistically, the majority of people who succeed in business have long-term goals in mind when they come up with new business ventures. It's also known that businesses will either succeed or crumble within the first five years. You don't open a business because you want instant gratification or to make money; in all honesty, you will likely lose money in the first couple of years. However, after ironing out the kinks and establishing a true vision, you have a better chance to succeed. I had the privilege to be on the *Kick Ass with Mel Robbins* audiobook and she told me, "Marques, most people get caught up in the weeds of the day-to-day and they don't time travel and set a vision. They aren't seeing into the future." She was so right. It's easy to get so caught up in the daily events and wins or losses that you don't realize the importance of time travel to where you really want to be and keep that vision in the forefront of everything you do. The vision is a key component of your drive, as it literally steers the directions you take.

In 2014, when Matthew McConaughey won the Oscar for Best Actor in *Dallas Buyers Club*, he gave an amazing speech. He started by thanking the Academy, all nominees, his director, and co-stars. He then talked about three things he needs daily. One is something to look up to. Another is something to look forward to. And the last is someone to chase. He then thanked God, because that's who he looks up to. He talked about the opportunities he feels have come from God. Then, he thanked his family, which is who he looks forward to. He talked about his parents, wife, and children and how he looks for reasons to make them proud.

Now, here's where you need to pay attention. He ended with thanking his hero, which is who he chases. He told a story about when he was fifteen years old, someone asked him who his hero was. He needed time to think about it, so the guy came back the following week and asked again, "Who is your hero?"

McConaughey replied that he had thought about it, and it was himself in ten years. When McConaughey turned twenty-five, the same person came to him and said, "So, are you your hero now?" to which McConaughey replied, "Not even close. My hero is me at thirty-five." Every day, month, year, the hero is always ahead, someone for him to chase. He is always ten years ahead of his life. He will continually chase himself, but ten years down the road. His vision is for ten years and will constantly change, but gives him the time and the ability to evolve and develop into who he wants to be.

I would say Matthew McConaughey has had a colorfully successful career, which his vision is a key component for. Get your mindset where you want to be, the faith of success. If you don't have the vision, you likely will lack drive and get stuck in the monotony of day-to-day life. I already discussed that, when I had my construction company, I had no drive. A huge part that was lacking was vision. I was all about the day-to-day. I wanted to get through the day, pick up a check, and go about my business. I was such a novice at success on a business level and lacked the training to create meaningful long-term successes. I had a C-level executive working as an estimator in my company. Looking back, he was probably the only one among us that truly had practiced the art of vision and time travel and knew the value of it. It was June of 2012 and he was the only one in our office repeatedly telling me I was focused on one particular job and not the growth of the company overall. I was so invested in a big-name job that was big for my ego that I put all my employees and finances into that job, as I felt it was going to be the job that propelled us to a bigger stage. He constantly told me to pull back a little bit and focus on other jobs and other ways the company could grow long term. I didn't listen to him. He ended up quitting a few weeks later and told me it was because he feared the company would not succeed with that mindset. Unfortunately, six months later, the job crumbled and my company was unable to sustain and closed down. He was absolutely, 100 percent right. I had no long-term vision and was focused on what made me feel good about myself, or my company, on the day-to-day. To sustain success, that's not how you operate and run a company.

This experience also taught me the value of having the right people on your team and trusting them to do the job you lay out for them to do. I did not listen to his expertise or value it. I put more faith in other people's opinions because that was what I wanted to hear.

I've learned the hard way that not only is it of extreme importance for you to have the vision, but also your team must have the right vision. Since I started re-branding myself, I have had so many people who wanted to align themselves with me. However, since I'm constantly changing and evolving, I expect the same of my team. My wife always says that some people are on our bus to success for a time period. They don't have the same destination in mind and will have to get off at various stops. Basically, she's saying that if people don't have the same ultimate vision in mind, or don't seek to evolve, then they don't need to be a part of the team for the long haul.

When I first started speaking, I didn't have a website. This is actually non-negotiable in the speaking field, but as a beginner, I was unaware and didn't have one. I aligned myself with a lady who hosted a website portal on which various speakers could advertise and send potential clients to for reference. She would also create contracts if you were able to book clients. It was kind of like a cattle call, and in some way might have done more harm than good, as prospective clients got to see other speakers as well. This was in no way what was beneficial for me long-term. This was not my ultimate vision as a speaker, to send prospective clients to a website that was not my own, for them to sift amongst several speakers until they found my bio.

However, as a beginner, while I figured out how to develop a team to create a website and earn the money to fund a website, this was what I had. Now, this lady was smart, taking advantage of an opportunity to create a portal to host potential clients and get paid to do so. But if I didn't have a vision to create something for myself, or to develop a team that worked with me exclusively, I would not have had the level of success I had. She was on the bus for a minute but was definitely not going toward our final destination. Her bus stop quickly approached.

Your power team should help set the vision, which is also an indicator of who shouldn't be on your team if they lack the vision or it doesn't align with yours and others on your team. If your power team isn't challenging you to set a bigger vision that is realistic, you don't have the right people on your team. When I started working with my current speaker manager, she did a complete diagnostic exam of our brand, from my website, to my marketing videos, and told me it would be harder for her to market my talents without the whole package at a level of excellence. She had a vision that challenged mine, but her vision was by far a better vision overall for the brand. It made me realize that, when you do have people on your team who are good at what they do and have the vision and want the growth, let them speak their thoughts into your company. Allow them to do what they are good at in order to enhance and create an even better way of achieving the overall vision. Trust them and you may be challenged to grow to make your own vision brighter than before.

It reminds me of Apple. I've seen many interviews with Steve Jobs, and he would always say he allowed healthy inclusion for the success of the company. Everyone has different tasks to achieve the goal, but the vision is the same. You then go on for years and see the success with each new vision. From iPads to AirPods, everyone was on board with the same vision, and Apple trusted their expertise to help create the successes needed to achieve it. A powerful vision pulls ideas, people, and other resources to create the energy to make it happen. It inspires people and natural leaders to persist and commit to give their best. A vision with purpose maintains the focus needed to achieve, especially in difficult or stressful times.

When developing your vision to sustain your drive, you should be clear and pay attention to the smallest detail. Many times, success lies in the detail, but also in the past mistakes. Be positive, understand that there are going to be difficulties and things may not go according to plan, or your vision has to change. Be open-minded and accept learning opportunities to improve upon. What if you don't achieve your vision? Don't let it derail you from evolving and starting again.

Create big visions, and give yourself and your team room to inspire and evoke energy. Don't allow your vision to be limited by what other people think or believe. Small-vision people lead small lives. Expand past your comfort zone and visualize the big opportunities and big accomplishments you are bound to experience.

Know your strengths and your weaknesses. Allow your team to know their strengths and weaknesses as well so you can empower each person's ability in the role they play and its importance in the overall vision. Know your role and that of your teammates. I cannot accomplish all the various things I need to in order to reach my brand's vision without my team. I simply do not have the time or the expertise. I had what I thought were good videos and an adequate website; my speaker manager disagreed. However, she was the one who knew what clients were looking for, and she also had the expertise to achieve the goal. Her strengths and detail were of that I wouldn't have had and plays to the overall vision of what we are trying to accomplish.

In our last chapter, we identified our *why*. We created our statements and understood what we were going to do to achieve the desired impact. With vision, we have to determine what our long-term future looks like.

Taking the tools above, I want you to use the following area to practice creating your vision.

- *Go for something big.* Thing about John F. Kennedy's vision to land on the moon; that was wild. That vision was huge and scary, but allowed the necessary push to make it.

- *Write from the heart.* Vision is about the future. What are your passions and desires for you and your company? Get excited. Indulge in what you have been told you can or even cannot achieve and let it guide you.

- *Jump to the future.* Write something as if you have already achieved it. Your brain is a powerful tool, and when you put things out there as if you have already accomplished them, your brain will spark to that. Write "we have" statements, not "we will."

- *Write now.* Don't wait until you have the perfect scenario played out in your head. Your vision may change, but put it out there now. Don't wait for things to happen first; put the pen to paper and get started. I would also suggest using a timed writing or hot pen technique. This allows you to write for a specific amount of time consistently, whether it's ten minutes or twenty. Do not pull your pen off the paper, just keep writing. Sometimes the most important parts of a vision are the ones people almost didn't write down.

- *Get personal.* It is OK to mix personal with professional in this aspect. Be bold and write down the elements of growth you would achieve through both.

- *Review, revise, and reach out.* Review your vision, make revisions as needed, and reach out to your power team for input and to make sure everyone is on the same page. The idea is to improve and create a clear understanding of the long term. It is important to share the vision with everyone that will be involved in bringing it to fruition. Your vision will set you all up to work together creating a common, encouraging, achievable positive picture of the future.

CHAPTER 10

Motivation vs. Inspiration

The last part that influences the drive is understanding the difference between motivation and inspiration and realizing how to implement them into your business plan. Motivation is derived from the word motive, which means I want you to do something for me because of what I get out of it. For example, I have to motivate my fifteen-year-old to clean her room. It doesn't bother her at all if her room is cleaned or not, but it drives me crazy. I motivate her, whether with an allowance or things she wants, to make her bed and clean her room. However, this is 100 percent for my satisfaction, not hers. It's also a short-term goal, since her room will most likely not stay clean for very long, and I will have to motivate her once again to clean it and repeat the cycle. You motivate someone to do something so that you gain from it. What happens from this? You will probably get what you want, but it might be met with hesitation, frustration, or even a sense of tiredness because it's not the other's goal.

However, inspiration is the act of breathing life into someone that makes them want a goal for themselves. For example, hopefully one day I will have inspired my fifteen-year-old to choose for herself to keep her room clean without looking for anything to gain. Inspiration creates long-term results. Inspiration is when you make someone want something for themselves, thus changing their actions or way of thinking to achieve their goal. Motivation breeds exhaustion and at times a sense of being overwhelmed, whereas inspiration pulls you toward something with a sense of easy energy and in an effortless way. I've heard it said before that motivation is the lazy man's tool, as they can't be bothered to get things done, where inspiration is a driving force or excitement to achieve something.

Culturally, we are motivated and not inspired. We need the quick fixes and instant gratification in life, the shortcuts, the immediate fulfillment, and we seek to achieve short-term goals, but we get burned out easily and give up. We don't always take the road less traveled and put the time into developing inspiration. Many times, people also don't allow themselves to be inspired because it might also cause more work. The motivated person has a time stamp on their work. They do what they need to in order to achieve someone else's goal, and then they are finished and move on. The inspired person is always seeking to gain more insight into inspirations and add to it, thus also creating a sense of more work; however, it will not be as difficult as it would be to work with just motivation. I've had people tell me for years that I am a workaholic. I agree. I am, but I have fun. I am inspired to be the best and create value, so what you see as long hours and being so busy, I see as a hobby, a lucrative hobby of networking and creating wealth while leaving a legacy for my family. I surround myself with like-minded people and watch how ideas become major accomplishments.

When you enjoy what you do (inspiration), you don't struggle with the actions of the day-to-day (motivation).

This concept is actually quite challenging to identify at times. When I first started speaking, I was motivated by money and motivated to teach others how to make money. I wanted to make money for a better life for my family. Why do any of us work? Because we need money to live right or to buy nice things, have a nice house, drive nice cars. There was nothing wrong with this, but it was so short-term. I would be motivated to get a speaking job. I would get the job, get paid, and then what? I would have to start over on the next job. I realized I was acting out of motivation and not inspiration. I was motivated by what others told me things cost. OK, you said I need $5,000 for a down payment on a truck I want; then I'm motivated to go get the job to pay for the truck. But I never created inspiration in what I was doing. I didn't know the difference, but when I learned, it clicked.

I wanted to lead a life of inspiration and let that navigate my drive. I really tried to identify what I wanted to do with inspiration being in the forefront. I changed my mindset and work ethic to inspire the creation of value for people and make a positive change for the community. This is long-term. When I focused on this inspiration, what happened? Money followed. My original motivation happened naturally when I was leading with inspiration. There is a Chinese proverb that says, "Man only has two legs and money has four." It means that, if man chases money, he will never catch up or be satisfied, but if you are focused on what you should be doing and focusing on the goal, money will always catch you. I was also not tired or mad when I didn't get something I was working toward. When I was driven by motivation, I would get so irritated when a speaking agency turned me down, or when a coaching client decided to hold off on coaching. Why? Because my motivation was money. It was a defeat. When I became focused on impacting the community and creating value, it no longer bothered me when I wouldn't land a job or a client needed to postpone their coaching ventures. My goal was still being met; I was still inspiring people to create value and making positive changes in the community.

In terms of your own business or brand, inspiration has to be part of the plan. If you look at successful leaders over time, they sought to inspire. Richard Branson has credited inspiration as the single most important leadership skill. So here we are, entrepreneurs, and we are a rare type of character: independent and willing to take risks in return for something unknown but possibly great. However, due to this, we often burn the candle at both ends. We need the inspiration to feed the drive. It's critical. Here are several ways to find your inspiration to take your drive to the next level:

- ▸ *Write it down:* Write down the good ideas, the bad ideas, the visions and the frustrations. Putting your thoughts on paper makes it easy to go back and find the diamonds in the rough. It will also allow you to see your thought patterns.

- ▸ *Read:* When you are not working, read. Read books, blogs, and anything else you can get your hands on covering the subject you are venturing into. Read about people in the field that you are seeking to get into, or even simply people you admire, and find the connections.

- ▸ *Move around:* If you work at home, or are stuck behind a desk all day, go to a coffee shop or even for a walk. Physical space impacts our thought process.

- ▸ *Travel:* Traveling is a great way to expand your horizons and see how the rest of the world lives. There is inspiration in finding people that do things in a different way than you or even discovering what was once unknown.

- ▸ *Ask:* Join a forum, ask people in the field questions. I've heard it said before, "The wise man doesn't give the right answers but poses the right questions."

- ▸ *Go to the gym:* This is huge for me personally. I am a self-proclaimed gym rat; however, I will say occupying my body can be stimulating to my mind. Focus on the strength of the body and often times you will see an increase of focus and endurance for what the day has in store. I know many former NFL players and business moguls who find their mental and physical release combined in yoga and meditation; alone with their breath, they find their inspiration, even if it's just for the tasks for that day.

- *Go on airplane mode:* Take a break from the world. I will be first to say sometimes this is easier said than done, but focusing on going for a walk or even having a meaningful conversation with someone will help clear out distractions in the mind.

- *Focus on yourself:* This one is hard for me at times. I have a wife and two kids, multiple business ventures, and my phone is constantly buzzing. It's hard for me to focus on myself, but taking care of yourself is very important. Get enough sleep, get a massage, take a vacation, indulge in the luxuries of life, and you will see that creativity is more naturally attainable.

- *Accept failure:* I cannot tell you how many lessons I have learned in my failed ventures. Our mess can become our powerful message. Our biggest failures can set us up for our biggest successes. I have the motto, "You win some, you learn some...I never lose some."

- *Be adaptable:* Learn to accept the imperfections and find value in them. Things aren't always going to go as planned but embrace the detour.

- *Evaluate your why:* Make sure your *why* is headed in the right direction and is strong enough to create an inspiration. It may need to change to allow for the inspiration to take flight.

- *Never stop learning:* Take a class, learn a language, go to a professional development seminar, and listen to lectures. The more you learn, the more opportunities you will have to discover new ideas.

▶ *Be creative:* I attended an NFLPA event with my wife. It was a sip-and-paint event encouraging us to creatively paint based off instructions. While I definitely didn't discover my long-lost artistic talents, it set an environment for my wife and I to discuss goals and ideas in our personal and professional lives while generating our visionary thinking.

▶ *Be dumb:* Not really, OK? Surround yourself with smart people. There is also value in being the dumbest person in the room. Surround yourself with experts in your area. They will not only lead by example, but will also push you to develop ideas and refine your path. I have so many people I continue to go to for advice, both in my field and in the business world in general. I always feel as if I leave with more ideas and more information than when I came, and that is very valuable to feeding my inspiration.

▶ *Keep it simple:* When I first moved to North Carolina after my business failed, I was going to hold elite football camps and try to get a job in construction to possibly open a construction company in Raleigh, and I had another idea for a business to bring networks of people together. I was all over the place, "Jack of all trades, master of none." Keep it simple. Focus on one thing at a time, get that started and running successfully before even considering another option.

▶ *Keep the small problems small:* Attack the small problems before they generate into larger problems. There is also value in using the problem-solving skills in the small things to connect to the larger.

▶ *Keep going:* I know the life of an entrepreneur can be exhausting at times, but just keep going. Be relentless in your business and planning. Get that second wind and run with it. Many times people quit right before they have success; just keep going.

Finding your inspiration and being inspired will propel you to countless possibilities and even change your own perception of your capabilities. You will likely not only find yourself through your inspiration, you will have the eagerness to achieve your goals and in turn will find successes based on these inspirations.

PART FIVE

HARD WORK

CHAPTER 11

It's Not a Nine-to-Five, It's a Ninety-five

I cannot tell you how many people I have talked to or even coached that get the ambition part down. They have their goals, they are willing to step outside the box and try new avenues of success and are even ready to create a road map or plan for success. These same people also identify their *why*, create a wild vision, and seek to inspire instead of motivate. They check off all the boxes that we have talked about so far, but still fail. Why? They never implement the hard work. To be quite honest, if you do all the other steps and then wonder why you aren't finding your success, it's because you are lazy in this area and aren't working hard enough. This is the time where you can't bullshit your way through the steps—you are either going to work or not. Your results will show through your action, or lack thereof. This is where I can identify who is all talk or who is serious about their business. Serious people don't miss meetings. They call when they say they are going to, and they go out of their way to create more innovative movements. These people are usually up early in the morning or late into the evening. These people live by their planner because they are so busy; they have to have something to organize their time.

There have been so many people that have come to me over the years and said, "I don't have time to work any more than I do. There aren't enough hours in the day." Yet these are the same people I see taking trips with friends, going out on the weekends, and lounging by the pool on social media. If you have time for any of that, you have time to work harder. We all have the same twenty-four hours in a day; how you use your time will result in your successes. It's just going to be down to how much you want it. It's also really important to identify early on the support of those close to you. My wife and I are both very similar with our vision, and we understand the amount of work that is involved in achieving our goals. If she was not supportive of me traveling all the time or being away from home in the evenings for events or meetings, filling the days and sometimes evenings with calls and meetings, my brand would not have become as successful as it has been. We have the same mindset. It helps that she is also very involved in what is happening with our business. We have been at dinners, movies, birthday parties, holidays, vacations, and other events where I had to step out to take a phone call from someone, or talk to a potential client because that was the time that fit their schedule. She was always on the same page; it's growing the brand. If she were the type of person that would become resentful of my time as I was growing our business, it wouldn't have worked. You have to have the talk about what working hard looks like with your spouse, partner, or loved one. Get them involved, let them know your goals and vision and where this hard work is going to take you. Everyone has to be involved in the support for success. How many hours extra a week are you working on the goals? Do you have set hours in the evening or weekends that you need? Let your spouse or partner know ahead of time so everyone is one the same page.

It's funny, the only time my wife ever got mad about me working was when our youngest daughter was born. We had a scheduled cesarean, which I was happy about. I put it in my planner and was ready to go. I was working several jobs at the time—football camps, one-on-one football coaching sessions, track out camps for kids, working on my first book—and had become involved in a sales position for a helmet company. This company had a lot of big contracts happening that day. Our time for delivery kept getting pushed back for emergencies, so I would step out to make a quick call, then come back in the triage while we waited. When it was finally go time, I went to the changing room to put on my scrubs, and my wife went into the operating room for her epidural. I knew my mother-in-law really wanted to be in the operating room, and I had managed while getting dressed to get the OK from the head of anesthesiology for her to come in, but she was in the waiting room several floors below us. I sprinted out of my room quickly and hurried downstairs to grab her and come back up. However, during this time, my wife's doctor was already making the first incision; they had come to get me, and I wasn't in the room. They went back to my wife and asked if she had anyone that would be in the room with her, to which she replied, "Of course, my husband is here." They informed her I wasn't in the room and she started yelling from the operating room for me—it wasn't nice yelling. She was strapped down on an operating table, hooked up to machines, and I'll tell you, when I got in the room, I was relieved that she couldn't come for me. She thought I stepped outside to make a phone call to a sales representative. I made it into the operating room in time; it definitely helped to have my mother-in-law in tow who could assure her I wasn't late because I was working. That was the only time my wife has said, "Turn the phone off." So of course, there are always exceptions to the rule. However, if you are starting a business or building a brand, you cannot think in terms of a forty-hour week.

When I say you are going to work, I mean you are going to *work*...maybe harder than you ever have before, and not for a short amount of time. You are going to work hard for years. I've heard entrepreneur Gary Vaynerchuk talk about how people come to him or email him all the time looking for his opinions. They tell him they have been working on their business on the side for a few hours every day and haven't had success. The only question he asks is, "How long have you been working on this business?" The average answer is between four to six months. To which he replies, "You haven't even begun to work hard yet. You are going to work hard for years." Success will be achieved but it's really a part of the never-ending journey. You won't work a nine-to-five job or a forty-hour week; it will be a ninety-five-hour week. If you are starting a new business or brand, don't quit your day job. Your day job will pay your bills; your hard work will create your success. Oprah always says you will do what you have to do so one day you can do what you want to do. This means you will come home from your normal job and work nights and weekends on your side hustle. You will miss happy hours, nights out with friends, impromptu trips. You will work on some holidays because you will be grinding. You will do this for years, and then little successes will begin to appear. I run into a lot of people—professional athletes, entrepreneurs—that don't understand that I always had a regular job while building. It's a sad call that I have had with way too many people who are down to their last one hundred dollars in the bank and are trying to build their brand but don't even have a job. That's unacceptable. I don't care if you are stocking shelves at a grocery store overnight, working security at a club or event venue, or waiting tables, you need a job. If you are looking to your new business or brand to fund your life-style, it won't. It will be *at least* a year, if not more, until you see the fruits of your labor. One criterion for me: unless you are funded properly, I won't take you on as a coaching client.

If you don't have a job that is securing your bills being paid, how can I expect you to work harder than you ever have when you aren't even working enough to pay your bills?

Many people say, "I want to work smart, not hard." It doesn't work like that. You have to work hard so that you can one day work smart. Opportunities will not fall in your lap, and if by chance that happened once, it won't necessarily happen again. I have a colleague that wanted to be a speaker. He booked his first speaking job for $5,000. Now, remember, when I wanted to be a keynote speaker, it took me two-and-a-half years to get paid, but here he was a couple months into it, earning $5,000. He thought, "Wow, this is amazing...let me get a few of these every month and I'll be happy." A year later he called me discouraged because he hadn't booked another event since the first one and didn't know what he was doing wrong. I told him how rare that was. He was a novice speaker with no speaking résumé, film, website, or referrals. He got lucky. That may happen once or twice, but it is not the norm. He then had to back up and reevaluate, take the steps to really create his brand in the speaking world, so that years later he won't have to work as hard, as people will seek him out on a regular basis.

I cold called people all the time for speaking jobs. I exhausted my inner circle and constantly asked people for referrals or favors. I was at every local speaker's bureau event and worked on my craft constantly. What happened? I started getting noticed. Over time, I formed a team of people so I had to do less—I was working smart—but no one on my team would have worked with me if I hadn't already achieved a certain level of success on my own. I got to the point where companies would seek me out instead of me calling them. Eventually, my hard work led to smart work, but it took years before that was even an option—almost four years to be exact. If you expect to succeed overnight, don't bother even starting.

So, why is hard work a part of the Success Cycle?

- ► *Because success isn't free.* If it were, everyone would have success. Success doesn't happen by chance, but by strategic actions.

- ► *Because hard work builds discipline.* When you first start your business or brand, you don't have the capabilities of handling all the responsibilities that come with it. Michael Phelps didn't earn several gold medals at the Olympics from his first race in the pool. He invested years of his life into the sport, hours training and getting his body and mind ready for the ultimate goal. Most millionaires didn't just become millionaires overnight. They learned how to manage their money, make specific investments, and network. There are steps to learn during the hard work that are vital for the success to last.

- ► *Because it's one of life's best teachers.* Hard work teaches you perseverance, the art of never giving up, appreciation, patience, responsibility, and purpose. You can't skip the line and expect to learn these things.

- ► *Because you make your own luck.* People that work hard don't sit around and wait for things to happen, they go out and make it happen.

► Because it gives you results. We measure things by progress, and consistent hard work breeds progress. Whether you are training for a marathon or trying to lose weight, seeing results makes you feel accomplished, and hard work gives you those results.

So, what should you do now to make sure you are working hard?

Number one, you should have a full-time job that is paying your bills. This is the first thing that is absolutely necessary. Don't let the success of a new business or brand be the stressor of your mortgage or electricity. You should always make sure you have a job that is funding your lifestyle before starting something new.

The second thing you should do is allocate how much time every week you are going to give yourself to work on your new business. This may change week-to-week or month-to-month given your schedule changes. You may have other responsibilities that limit you one week or one month, but make you more available at other times. If you could give yourself at least two hours every night and ten hours over the weekend, that is an additional twenty hours a week you are pouring into your success. Have office hours and identify what you are doing during those hours, whether it is meeting with people, responding to emails, or working on content or your website. I have a coaching client who I talk to every week. He uses his lunch hour from his regular job to meet with me for the personalized steps to grow his business. Here he is finding the nuggets of time throughout his day to pour into creating his dream. Also, I want to make it clear, working specific extra hours doesn't mean you are now no longer available to your family. I cannot tell you how many phone calls I have taken while sitting in my four-year-old's room having a tea party, or how many emails I have sent to clients while watching *Frozen* or driving a car full of kids from one activity to another. You can still be present while working. Document it, let your family be a part of the goal, and celebrate together too. My four-year-old loves to think she is helping me work by playing quietly while I'm on a call.

The third thing is to have a big vision, but focus small. You cannot overlook the small details in creating your company. Rome wasn't built in a day, and neither will your business or brand. If you are a big-project-minded person, but not a detail person, that will not produce a quality product or business. You have to focus on all elements. When I started out in speaking, I had a basic website. It served a purpose for me to send potential clients somewhere they could see reviews and information, but the site was all over the place. It was overcrowded and lacked clarity and information. It was hard to follow and disorganized. My website had to be perfected in a more detailed manner for higher quality clients to take me seriously. I couldn't be a great keynote speaker without first taking care of the smaller areas of focus. What are your areas of focus that you have possibly overlooked? Is it your website? Is it your attire? Your presentation? Your ability to connect with people? Your marketing?

Is it the value your business or brand provides? Identify those areas and spend time working on them.

The fourth thing you should be doing is talking with people. Networking is a huge part of success. Surround yourself with people who are also working hard on their ideas and you will feed off of each other's energy. The Rock always says that regardless if he is working out, working on movies, in business meetings, or producing movies through his production company, he strives to be the hardest working person in the room. He isn't saying this from an arrogant standpoint, but from a "let's get shit done" position. He aligns himself with people that also have that mindset, and guess what? They get shit done. He has the number one ranking of any actor on social media and is finding himself on the list of one of the highest paid actors in Hollywood...all by being one of the hardest working persons in the room and surrounding himself with others like that. Networking is huge and is necessary in growing a successful business.

CHAPTER 12

Focus on You, Not Your Competition

Everyone has an idea of how they think success works. If you haven't already figured it out, the life of an entrepreneur is exciting one minute, when you think everything is working great, only to hit you like a ton of bricks the very next minute, when things feel like they are falling apart and you question why you ever decided to step out on your own. The reality is, the road to success isn't easy, and it's different for everyone. Actually, the only thing I can promise is that it will not be what you expect.

This chapter is about focusing on you and not your competition in two ways. The first way is to build your own brand and

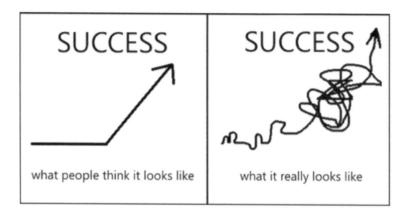

business without getting sidetracked on other people's successes. The second way is to stay in your lane without getting derailed. We will talk about that one in a bit, but for now let's talk about the first. I've already told you that you will fail many times and sometimes even for years. You have to go into this expecting to fail sometimes. When you consider that you won't win at every moment on the ride, you will be able to handle the journey a lot better. The truth is, my colleagues, readers, audiences, and clients only see the areas I succeeded in. However, the reality is I failed a lot. I can name five failed businesses off the top of my head that I was involved with in the past five years. They failed for different reasons, and all were contingent on other people doing their part of the business as well, but things don't always go according to your plan, and that's OK.

Most entrepreneurs are hard on themselves. Competition is tough in the business world, and it's easy to compare yourself to your competition any chance you get. You have to stop the comparison; it only affects you. As I mentioned in the last chapter, at this time in your business, you are going to work hard—for some of you, harder than you ever have. You are going to be pouring your blood, sweat, and tears into pursuing your passion. In doing this, it's going to be really easy to want to take shortcuts here and there, or to watch other people succeed faster and get hindered in your own work. You have to mindfully stop and focus on yourself and work on perfecting your business or craft. I think back to the Matthew McConaughey story we talked about earlier. He was constantly chasing his future self. If you compete with anyone, let it be your brand or business in the future. You've laid out the vision, made the road map, and have the mission of what you want to do and how you want to do it; now, get to it. Don't let other people's directions trip you up. Don't drain yourself and your energy focusing on what everyone else is doing better than you. When you focus on others, you lose some of your creative edge, fire, and desire to succeed. I understand this is sometimes easier said than done. I was left with my jaw on the floor when my colleague who just started in the speaking industry got the job for $5,000 within his first couple months, while it took me years to get paid a lot less than that. However, I couldn't focus on that. I had to bring my attention back to my specific brand and mission and pour my energy into that. It is also OK and important to know your market, to acknowledge and gain insight into trends that are successful or not in your developing business, but don't worry about others' quarterly income, endorsements, clients, or opportunities. It will only strip you of your potential.

If you are constantly watching your competition and comparing successes, you are absolutely not going to reach your potential. You are going to miss it. I remember a *Will and Grace* episode I watched years ago where Grace wanted a personal trainer, but didn't want to spend the money, so she secretly followed a girl and her trainer around the gym and did the same exercises. After a couple months she got caught and began to tell the trainer he wasn't very good because she felt her butt was getting bigger, when the trainer said, "That was my client's goal, for her butt to get bigger." If you are so caught up on your competition, you will lose your goals and vision and accept theirs without even knowing what they are. You have to stay focused on your goals and vision. Keep that vision board or mission statement where you can see it daily. Remind yourself of your *why* because everyone's is different.

I have colleagues in the speaking community who are very happy and satisfied with one or two speaking jobs a month. I have had people tell me that if they can bring in $3,000–$5,000 a month, they are fulfilled and content. That's great. It's absolutely wonderful that they know what they want and have their monthly goal they strive for. For myself, my monthly goals are much bigger than that, so if I were comparing myself to them, without even knowing what they were striving for, I would fall short of my own goal every month and be extremely frustrated. The reality is, most of your competitors aren't going to tell you what they want to make per month or how much extra time they are working on something, so you will never know and always wonder why they are so content and you feel that you have failed or fallen short. Focus on you, your *why*, and your goals. Focus on what works and what doesn't for your specific brand.

In the chapters above, I touched on the importance of "being the dummy." Surround yourself with smart people in the industry and learn from them. This is different than focusing on your competition. These are mentors, coaches—people who are not your competition because they have already succeeded at what you are trying to do. These are the ones lighting the path for you. It's not only smart, but also essential to align yourself with people who have *made it* in their industry. They will teach you, they will coach you, they will cheer for your success—they are not your competition.

The truth is, there's enough business out there for everyone. This is where your energy and time need to be spent. This is where focusing on your brand and business is vital. Find the value that you and your product bring to the industry you are seeking to embark on. For me as a speaker, I had to remember what Tony Robbins always said in those podcasts I listened to while cleaning out office buildings: *everyone has a story; find your story.* I had to focus on my story, make it different, make it relatable, and seek to find connections. The same goes for you. Are you trying to be a speaker? Reveal a new product? Open a brokerage firm? Whatever your goal and vision is, know your story, know your worth, and focus on that.

The second part of this chapter is about staying focused on you and your brand in a different way. When I first moved to North Carolina from Baltimore, my construction company had just declared bankruptcy. I had lost everything—my title, my ego, my 3,000 square-foot office space, multiple trucks, millions of dollars in money, my home, multiple cars, and even my cell phone. The list could go on and on, but I think you get the idea. I was strapped for cash and wanted so badly to be relevant again, to feed my ego and become successful. I had so many random ideas, from football camps, to radio hosting, to another construction company, and so on. I created a business called Collective Networks that would make introductions between networks for people looking to do business with others. I had a potential lead to work in the pharmaceutical business, as well as the sports apparel and safety businesses. I owned and operated a seven-on-seven football league. Long story short, I was all over the place. I had no real focus and was throwing all my ideas against a wall to see if anything would stick. Clearly, not many of them did. I had no focus on any one area and was running around like a chicken with his head cut off. I was tired and couldn't keep meetings and ideas straight. Nothing was successful or worth the amount of time and work I was putting into it. There were no long-term possibilities for some of the ideas.

Then I decided to become a speaker—another thing to add to the list, right? My wife told me to stop anything that wasn't bringing money in and focus on one lane. I was working hard but not smart. I was giving my time and energy to too many areas, but if I were just to pour that energy in one direction, it had a more likely chance to succeed.

I see this happen all the time. People are throwing things out to see which one is their ticket to success. Pick a lane and stay in it. Master one area before adding another. Don't focus on what someone else is doing in a different field, focus on what you are doing and growing in your field. I did this. I focused on speaking. It took time, but during that time, I was able to master certain areas to create revenue while staying in my lane of keynote speaking. I released my first book. I wanted to release that book to share my story with people, but also to create credibility in the speaking world. It was a way clients could learn about me, and guess what? I could make money off it. I started having people reach out to me, asking how I became a speaker, so I started a speaking academy. It was a two-day workshop for people to learn the basic things they needed to embark on a speaking career, from what their website should look like, to social media, to what types of slides they should create, to how they should develop an elevator pitch, to what types of questions they will be asked. I brought people in that were successful in those areas to teach. I had my web designer come in and discuss trends and what the market looked like for speakers. I created value while staying in my lane and making money in a different way than just speaking. From this, I also created even more credibility for myself as a speaker, and began booking more events. I also started developing one-on-one coaching sessions, helping people not just with speaking, but also with leadership, sales, marketing, and branding. My brand started to expand, but was always staying relevant to the original lane. Focus on your lane; focus on the legs that can grow off of your legs that are still relevant to your original goal. I had to let go of football camps, football leagues, football coaching, merchandising sales, and sports radio. They weren't conducive to my focus area. At this time, my original focus is in stride, it's established and working on its own so that I can introduce other opportunities. When you are working on one goal, stay completely concentrated on it.

Similar to seeing people fixated on other things outside their lane, I see people focused on if they compare to the successes of others. I have clients that live in areas of the country where it's not uncommon to see people riding around in Bentleys, dripping in diamonds, and living a life of luxury. Imagine you are a realtor trying to sell homes or a financial investor trying to gain people's trust financially, and you are driving a "regular" car. But the person down the street selling homes or with that new brokerage firm is driving the brand-new Bentley, Ferrari, or Mercedes. That may make you have a sense of self-doubt, right? You suddenly start thinking, "I'm not as successful as they are because I don't have a new car or custom suit." You cannot worry about your environment. You can't compare because you can't control it. It's extremely important that when you are focusing on yourself, you don't get distracted by what it appears other people have. I cannot tell you how many people I have met that have brand new everything, their kids go to the most expensive private schools, and so on, but their credit cards bounce when they are trying to pay for a hundred-dollar football camp or a five-hundred-dollar coaching session. These same people can't even get gas for those cars they are showing off. I can tell you story after story of former NFL players that had huge contracts, that you would think had all their ducks in a row, that would have money for life, only to become homeless or go on welfare later on in life. You cannot worry about your competition's success or the results of their success. Focus on what you need to do to achieve your own success without being clouded by what others have, or seem to have.

CHAPTER 13

Building Your Power Team

At some point during the long hours, when your business or brand is starting to grow, you will realize you cannot physically and mentally do everything needed for the continued growth. You will hit a wall. You also will identify your areas of strength and your areas of weakness. This is when you will need to start looking for your power team. A power team is a group of professionals working together in non-competing fields in relation to the same vision. Building your power team can be nerve-racking. Who can you trust? Who is honest with their résumés or capabilities? These people are representing you and your brand. Are you really comfortable with the type of people they are to represent you in a professional manner?

I think back on my time with my construction company. I had absolutely created the wrong power team. I had people working for me who falsified their résumés. I had people who were lazy with questionable work ethics and morals. I had people who overstepped their areas of work and tried to control other areas. In reality, the one person on my team who was forthcoming and honest was someone I overlooked. He ultimately quit and my team went from bad to worse in a matter of weeks. Overall, I was responsible for employing and creating the wrong team. I cannot stress enough the importance of your team. They will either aid your success or your failure.

When I moved to North Carolina and started over, my team was small. It was me and my wife. Honestly, we felt we couldn't trust anyone else and were scared. However, as we continued to grow as a business, we were capped out at what we could do. We had to develop a team, but where to start? If you are starting any type of company or branding from the ground up, you need these basic four people on your team initially.

You need a lawyer. You need someone to incorporate the business the right way and to help you understand the laws surrounding the business you are in.

You need an accountant. You need someone who will make sure everything is in place for taxes. Personally, this is not my area of strength, and I knew I didn't want to miss anything in relation to the IRS, so this was vital for me. However, if your business is small enough, you may be confident to punch the numbers yourself. For me, it was very important to incorporate an accountant early on.

You need a business banker. You have to set the business up correctly and run things in and out appropriately. Your business banker and accountant will talk about write-offs and how to keep things structured.

Finally, you need a web designer. You need someone who is able to get your thoughts across as well as your services or products somewhere to drive clients to.

With these four areas above, this is the beginning of your power team. It will grow from here. My power team has changed in those four areas alone around three to four times since I first started. As my brand grew legs and ventured into bigger visions, I had to make sure my power team was also aligned and capable of the responsibilities with the new vision. Over time, as my successes began to grow, I added to my team and started looking for speaker agents, marketing and advertising strategists, videographers, social media specialists, graphic designers, assistants...the list goes on.

I cannot stress enough the vital importance of trusting your team. These are the people who are talking to others on your behalf, representing you, and working to grow your image and brand. Along with myself, my human-resources manager (HR) has always been my wife. This person is going to vet people. They are going to do background checks and make sure people are who they say they are. Personally, I feel this person has to be the one that you trust the most. This position focuses on the others and levels the risk of involvement.

About two to three years after I started speaking, I began a speaking academy. I had a lot of people—former ballplayers, regular entrepreneurs—that would ask me tips and advice for breaking into the speaking field. I decided I would hold an academy and provide a two-day experience filled with the basics of what worked for me, what didn't, and so on. At this time, I had someone who had just joined my brand to represent me as a speaker agent. I didn't really do my homework on the person, but at the same time, I didn't have much to lose because I was the only one out there getting myself jobs, so if he could add to that, then I was happy. He saw what I was doing with the academy and desperately wanted to be a part of it. His approach was, "Hey, let me help you...you don't have anyone besides your wife really helping. I've done things like this before and can totally be of assistance."

I thought this would be great. Neither my wife nor I had ever hosted an academy type of event, so I was grateful for the help. As time went on, he would send me locations he found. He then would send me potential itineraries and people he thought would be good to speak at the event. I was so busy with other things, I didn't focus too much on what he was doing, trusting he wasn't making any specific decisions without me, as these were just topics to discuss. One afternoon while working, my wife intercepted an email from him. She started digging into other things and found out he not only had contracted a hotel without approval but had also booked people to speak at the event. She did more digging and found the ones he booked had no speaking experience, but were actually other clients of his, so he would be getting a kickback. She came to me with all this information of flights and hotels he promised his team we would be paying for, photographers he booked without consent, and so forth. When I brought it to his attention, he reacted with, "I don't have a working relationship with your wife; either she goes or I go." I'm not sure if anyone reading this is married, but that's not really an ultimatum you give, especially in my case. He and I ended our relationship immediately, as he knew we would find more inconsistencies with his stories as we continued. He was planning to show out for his friends he was bringing to our academy on our dime to help run the event. During this time he never brought any of this to our attention, nor did he do any of the speaker management duties he was originally brought in to do. I'm not telling you this story to highlight a certain person, but to tell you that not everyone on your team is there for the right reasons. You may have to weed through the garbage to find the right fit. It's part of the learning process. I'd like to say since then I have learned everything I need to know and it's been smooth sailing. That's not the case.

There have been people that want to be a part of the brand, but for whatever reason, our time together doesn't last. I work long hours and expect the same out of my team. I have had people be a part of the team that just couldn't work the same way. I get it, and I don't fault them for it, but I don't slow down for anyone when it comes to the direction of my brand and my vision. When I say this, I do know I am not just working for myself. As much as someone is on my team, I'm a part of their team. If I have social media strategists on my team, I want my content or success to be able to help them gain new clients as well. I have assisted many on my power team with closing deals or gaining new clients. In regard to a power team, I always say it's like a bus route. People may get on board at the very beginning with you but they aren't going to the same destination. They are going to get off the bus before you, but at the same time, you will be picking other people up along the way that are headed where you are going. Some people are only on the team for a period of time and that's OK.

As I said before, I went through several people in various fields before finding the right ones for my team. I have gone through four web designers in five years before finding the one that has my vision and can cast it in a way that grows the brand. I have gone through several accountants—as my brand grows, so does my financial situation. Things get more complicated. I have to know the person can handle the ins and outs of the situation, while educating me along the way. I have gone through at least four to five speaking agents before finding the one right for my specific needs.

So think about this: other than the necessary areas of legal, accounting, and banking, there are four key areas when it comes to building your power team. These are people you will work with daily. In those key areas, you are involved in each one. You are learning from the professionals you put in those areas, but you are never absent. The four areas are:

> *Marketing and brand development:* The people in this field are the ones putting out marketing leads, whether that's through social media content, newsletters, film,

or surveying marketing trends and implementing them with our mission in place. These people are the ones getting the potential client's attention. They have to be evolving with the trends, studying the successes of what is working, and evaluating what is not.

▸ *Sales development and awareness:* The people in this field are taking the leads through our marketing team and putting them into action. They are contacting leads and negotiating contracts, financials, and logistics of action. They have to not only be aware of the marketing that was used to get the attention of the potential client but also what the promised delivery is capable of. They have to be able to sell the product or service with the knowledge of it fulfilling the client's needs.

▸ *Human resources and hiring:* These are the people who vet new people on the power team. They are the ones who try to make sure certain people will best represent your brand or business, from social media posts to actually being capable of doing the job they are trying to obtain. They are the ones that check the résumés or references. They check the track record and what people have said about working with others. They are typically the ones checking compliance and safety in the information going out.

▸ *Productions area:* These are the ones that are actually doing the work for the company or brand. For myself as a speaker or coach, this would be me. I'm the one actually delivering on the coaching sessions or keynote speaker. This person is typically the face of the business.

Probably, if you are reading this book, you will find not only are you a part of each of the sections, but this is your main spot. You are the CEO, responsible for the growth or decline of the business.

When you are developing your power team, you need to keep these key areas in mind. Write them out. Who do you have in those areas? Are those areas strong or weak? Are there changes that need to be made? Is everyone on board? Not only are you responsible for knowing your strengths and weaknesses, you should know the strengths and weaknesses of your team. Are they seeking to gain more knowledge in their areas of expertise, or have they plateaued and are fine where they are? Are they onboard when you seek to add another leg to your brand or business?

Your power team is a key component of your success. Everyone has the same amount of time in a day, but not one person can do all the things needed to succeed in one day. As your business grows, so will your team. It's growth in and of itself. Find people who are experts in their field, people you trust and have the same vision. Find people that take not only the company image but also your image in mind when working. Find people that are eager to expand their network and excited to work. Find people who collaborate well with others and create an environment where everyone feels like an important member of the team. So, once you have your team, what is needed to make it truly powerful?

▶ Leadership that inspires them to act. Help them feel valued in their line of expertise.

- ▶ Vision: everyone has to have the same vision they are working toward.

- ▶ People who are encouraged to share their ideas or thoughts in a comfortable environment, as well as accept feedback.

- ▶ An understanding of others' roles in the team. This is not a one-person show; there are checks and balances and many roles to complete the mission.

- ▶ A judgment-free zone. Whether you agree or disagree with ideas or opinions, keep it judgment-free.

- ▶ People who aren't seeking all the credit or glory.

- ▶ Once a decision or plan of action is decided, everyone jumping on board in a positive way.

- ▶ A team leader leading by example with the encouragement of others seeking first to understand, then to be understood.

If you can create these qualities while creating your power team, you will eliminate who shouldn't be there, while adding value to those who should. This is in and of itself hard work, but the successes to come with your power team are by far greater than what you could accomplish alone.

CHAPTER 14

Multiple Streams of Income

Chances are the majority of people reading this book are or are trying to become entrepreneurs. One common aspect among entrepreneurs is many of them have, or desire to have, multiple streams of income. The reality is, being an entrepreneur is tough. It's a roller coaster of emotions ranging from being on top of the world one moment to wondering why you ever decided to jump down the rabbit hole of chaos the next. Expect the stress. Everyone has stress, it's a part of life, but *entrepreneur stress* takes it to a whole new level. The responsibility to not only provide for yourself, but also for your business and employees monthly can be quite overwhelming. This is why multiple streams of income are imperative.

What if you are a one-income household? What happens if you lose your job? Do you have six months of living expenses paid for in your savings? Many of us do not. In reality, many of us are in a two-income household and still don't have that amount in savings. In my opinion, I feel like whether you have a nine-to-five, two-income household or are starting a new business, creating multiple streams of income will not hinder you in any way.

When I moved to North Carolina, I immediately created a few streams of income. I was coaching athletes in my backyard, running football camps, and working as a janitor. I didn't create these to get ahead, but I wasn't making enough in each of these positions alone to pay my bills. However, I saw the value of having multiple sources of revenue early on. I realized then that if I were to build various sources of income that I would more than likely be protected. What if the market goes into a recession again? What would likely be the first thing people cut back on? Extracurricular activities. This would mean that I would have one less source of revenue, and possibly two, with the need for one-on-one training and football camps ceasing. I knew that to live a lifestyle I wanted to live, while also creating a savings plan, going on vacations, putting money away for taxes and so on, I needed six to eight legitimate streams of income.

I know you might think it just sounds easy to create the different streams of income, but that's not the case. Some ideas never work out (a true entrepreneur issue), and others are for around for a good time, not a long time. However, in the midst of all this, I was able to establish several lines of revenue over the years. Within the past five years, I have created ten streams of income, some of which are extremely lucrative, from keynote speaking, executive coaching, consulting, and book revenues, to others that are seasonal, like one-on-one football training. However, what I know is that in having these various avenues, I have not only created a variety of wealth, but also enhanced my brand and company overall.

So whether you are a nine-to-five corporate America guru or an entrepreneur, I see no downside in creating multiple streams of income.

What I found these past few years is that I was building job security for myself. The traditional mindset of waking up early, driving to work, climbing the corporate ladder, and retiring no longer applies to many people. Jobs are being outsourced or replaced overall. Companies are hiring for temporary positions instead of company employees for a myriad of reasons. Creating a safe haven of job security for you and your family is unfortunately a real thing you have to consider. When you think about the world we live in and the simplicity that technology has created for us, it is a real thing to consider the likelihood of job security being a viable question in the minds of many of our everyday workers. Just take Amazon in the retail world. Since the launch of Amazon Prime and Amazon Prime Now, traditional retail stores like Nordstrom, Macy's, Best Buy, and others have announced layoffs and are struggling with in-store retail decline. However, at the same time, technology makes it possible to create various sources of revenue from your home, whether it is through self-starting businesses or services to network marketing. Because of the diverse opportunities online, online business owners can tap into a variety of markets, creating potential job opportunities, and each will create more job security for those looking.

Multiple streams of income also allow you to create opportunities for yourself. You may have a full-time job that you love, but creating a new opportunity for yourself and your family will not only build your résumé in a new way, but also give you the opportunity to pursue passions, whether through your new side hustle or from income from that opportunity. I hear from various people all the time about being not only afraid to start a new source of revenue, but also being tired. I get it. You have to know you will work hard, but it will eventually produce for you and your family. I encourage people to initially keep it relative to what you know. If you are a realtor, you may find you want to buy a beach rental property as a second source of income. It's relative to what you know and have mastered. Years ago, as a speaker, I was able to create another viable source, but stay in the arena I was confident in by creating a speaking academy. That led to executive coaching, which led to consulting and brand ambassador opportunities. As time goes on, you may find the desire to diversify and venture into other types of income sources but keeping it relative to what you know is key in the beginning.

Another reason why multiple streams of income is key is it allows you to stick to your values and beliefs. I speak to so many millennials, and often what they are known for is not compromising their beliefs or morals. I thought about this and what it means in our world. So many people I have coached or spoken with have shared stories with me of having been faced with the decisions to either sacrifice their integrity or quit the corporate world. Having something to fall back on, and being able to rely on yourself, extinguishes that issue. Being able to pursue your passion, grow a business, and live life by your own set of morals and values means less stress and a deeper satisfaction. I see this all the time, not only with my wife and me, who do a lot of our work from home, but also from other people who have work-from-home businesses. This allows parents to stay home with their kids, or to work from anywhere, travel the world, and still enhance their brand and business appropriately.

Having multiple streams of income allows you to take risks. I absolutely promote initially staying in your lane. As I said earlier, if you are a realtor, maybe a second source of income would be buying a vacation rental property. However, sourcing multiple streams of income can create the opportunity for eventually stepping out and being daring. Do something you haven't done before, take risks, and possibly reap an amazing reward. In some situations, the time to take risks is when you are younger or don't have a lot of extra responsibilities. When you are married with three kids, a mortgage, and college on the horizon, you need to be safe. Things get harder when you have family and obligations, and failure always hangs in the back of the entrepreneur's mind, but when you are young, failure has fewer repercussions. So, with this said—millennials, I'm talking to you—build revenue sources so you may take risks and have fun learning along the way. Of course, in saying this, I would never tell anyone they are too old to take risks if they so choose.

Years ago I was at my in-laws' house and my wife's grandfather was sitting at the table and asking me about business. I told him I feel like I'm working all the time and just trying to make sure what I am doing is worth all the work. He laughed and said, "You're in your thirties; you should be working all the time." It was such a commonsense response from him, but it made me realize that he was right. The time to pour myself into my work and really create was when I was young, with the energy to match. You need energy to build a business, let alone multiple businesses creating income. I only wish I would have had this mindset in my twenties. When you have the energy, utilize it, and create the sources of income to take you into your latter years with ease.

Another huge reason to create multiple streams of income is for tax benefits. New tax cuts and job acts actually benefit people who receive income through self-employment through online or work-from-home jobs. This is where your accountant can really find the up-to-date benefits for your specific work. Having multiple streams of income is also a great way to pay taxes. So many times we find ourselves with huge tax bills and have to pay them off over a number of years. Building a nest egg for taxes or emergencies through multiple streams can only assist in the demand.

I also know several people who are using their multiple income streams to source their retirements. Unfortunately, gone are the days where you would work twenty to twenty-five years with a company, knowing that you will be taken care of until you die. You need a retirement plan. We see this with the baby boomers who are working later into their retirement years because there is no retirement there to take care of them. What if you could retire at your own pace, instead of what your 401(k) dictates? When I think of young adults and entrepreneurs, I can't help but hope they are already dealing with their long-term financial plans. Between student loans that are on the rise, and a constantly changing job market with multiple outsourcing issues, it is imperative to become self-reliant. Pensions are a thing of the past and this is why it's ever more important to continue to create multiple streams of income.

So many people I coach or talk to always tell me they can sometimes barely plan for next week, let alone think about building for long-term wealth. However, the fact is, the more work you put in now with a side hustle or online business or service, the more likely your long-term effects can be enormous with capital gains. Having your regular job and then building others to self-sustain themselves will build long-term wealth without the headache of trying so hard. It does take a considerable amount of work to get there, though. Don't quit your day job. Don't rely on a side hustle. Let it be an extra source of revenue that builds for you and your family. You will find that being able to no longer trade time for money in the future will allow you to focus on what's really important in your life.

So where do you go from here? There are several common sources of extra income. For most people, their primary salary is their main income stream. Most people start this way. Let this pay your bills, while you create something to add to your wealth. Max out your primary salary by getting yourself in the position to be the most valuable at what you do, whether that's through professional development, coaching, accreditations, or climbing the corporate ladder. Once you are there, you can start adding to your primary source. Many people's second source of income is a spouse or partner's salary. Gone are the days where we live in a typical one-income family, and not only for monetary reasons—we are globally placing value on our careers in a sense where partners like to work and feel a part of a bigger field of study. I'm a big believer in teamwork. Having a spouse or partner who also works creates a sense of security should anything happen to one of your primary incomes.

Many people go from their career jobs to investments. Investing, whether into a stock or bond or into a tangible item like a second home, can only add to your overall wealth. For most, it's saving for retirement, but it could likely become an emergency fund as well. If you choose the tangible items like a rental property over investing in stocks and bonds, you will have some related expenses that would differ, such as mortgage, utilities, property tax, and overall upkeep of the house. However, rental properties do have tax advantages that investing doesn't have.

Another form of multiple streams of income would be through online businesses/services or hobby business. This is where I find the majority of my multiple streams derive from. This is the side business. This could be online or offline. We live in a high technology world with enhanced social media platforms to take our businesses wherever we want to go globally. The world is fast-paced, changing constantly, and the people who can adapt with the times are going to be the ones who achieve maximum success and prosperity. The amazing thing about social media is you can double dip with websites like Fiverr.com or others like it. If you have a skill, you can put your skill out there for people to see, or if you are looking for a particular skill, it can be purchased through the same site. Anything is possible, from creating social media content for your brand to hiring or even being available as a virtual assistant.

The point is, you can diversify your income in various ways to maximize your successes overall. After you have established your primary source, take each additional source one at a time. Get that next source in full swing, whether it's an online company or service, a rental home, or whatever. Follow the Success Cycle for each business venture until it is a well-oiled machine running on its own, then introduce another. You don't have to be super rich, and you don't need a lot of time to get started. You can work your job, find a side hustle, invest your money, or buy a rental property and go from there. The reward is great but the action to take the first step is required.

PART SIX

REPEAT
THE CYCLE

CHAPTER 15

Set New Goals

W hen will you know if the Cycle worked and you are successful? Go back to that original goal. Did you meet it, or
are you within sight of it? Are things getting easier and falling
into place? Are you ending phone calls feeling encouraged
instead of discouraged? Are you making the right connections
and building a team of people that have a reputable name in
their industry? Have you started to see a return on your investment? Remember, you will likely not see the success for the
first few years. Within three to five years, you will start to see
if things are working, or if you need to pivot. This is when you
will know if the Cycle is working or not. If not, go back through
the Cycle and find the issues and correct the problems or issues
to get back on course. If it is, then what?

So let's imagine you have followed the pattern. You have established your ambition through setting realistic goals, stepping out of your comfort zone, and establishing your path or road map to achieve those goals. You have moved on to the drive, where you identify your *why*, your vision; you have distinguished your long-term inspirational desires versus your short-term motivational outtakes; and you are able to implement your inspirational desires into your daily courses of action.

Accompanying your ambition and drive is your hard work. You have put the plans in motion, understanding you will be working extra hours on nights and weekends to fund your vision, staying in your lane, competing with only yourself, building your power team of professionals around you, and establishing multiple streams of income. What next?

Repeat the Cycle.

So many times, I see people have success with this program, then just flake off. You have to have the mindset that success is never over. If you find you achieved success in one area, then go back and add another goal and start the process over. Complacency is the enemy of progress. I think back to when I had my construction company. I had a goal and achieved it within my first four years. However, I never set a new one. I was overconfident. I felt like I was at the top and was happy where I was. I lost it all the very next year and ended up filing Chapter 7 bankruptcy. I see this happen a lot. People celebrate their accomplishments and go on vacation, take a break from working hard. Three months turns to six months, and then to a year, and then suddenly, you not only haven't created anything new, but your once successful venture might not be as successful anymore. You have to always grow into the next chapter of your business, whether that is adding to a service that you are already successful at or starting a totally different venture. You always have to be looking forward. This is also imperative for the long-term success of your company or business. What does the business world look like? What are the changing tides in technology and consumerism? You have to constantly grow into the next realm of what is working in the business world to stay relevant.

This also helps with establishing multiple streams of income. When you have one area of success and you feel like that area gets to a point of being self-sustainable or not requiring as much of your attention and time, that is when you are ready to start something new. Start a new goal. This could be branching a leg off of an already established goal or something new entirely. For example, after I established myself on the speaker circuit and became successful in that arena, I then decided to focus on other ventures that were related: executive coaching and consulting. They were similar to speaking, but different. I was using many of the same techniques I knew from speaking to assist with the new execution of the executive calls and consulting. You may find yourself interested in a completely different field as well. I get approached all the time to consult or invest in construction companies, specifically site work and dirt work, since that was my field of expertise with my former company. I built the company into being the top minority-owned construction company in the city of Baltimore in a matter of years. I know what works and what doesn't. I also have experience in the failure of that company to be on the lookout for potential problems. This is a realm completely separate from my speaking career. It doesn't matter if you find you want to stay in the same realm of what you do or venture out into a new one. Start at the beginning and follow the Cycle so that you don't slide down a slippery slope of complacency.

If you do find you are stuck and aren't sure what to do next, consider these strategies:

- *Set a bigger goal:* This could be an expansion of the first goal. The Cycle is endless with this option. Keep grinding into something bigger and better, even if it's just making yourself the goal. Learn something new in your field, professional development, a new trade that will set you and your service or company apart from others.

- *Move the original goal out:* This is similar to the strategy above, but instead of making a bigger goal, give yourself time to expand on the original one. For example, if a person has a goal to run a half-marathon, maybe they will now consider a full marathon.

- *Identify other personal passions:* Use a new goal to identify other passions you may have outside your field, whether this is learning to surf or getting into radio and television. Identify other passions and the possibilities that may lead to opportunities.

- *Quit:* I can't believe I put that out there myself, but learn to stop when you are ahead. In the sports world, you have so many people that try to stay as long as they can, but some players are washed up and old. Retire when you are ahead. So, this means maybe you have written a few bestseller books but aren't sure about a third...quit while you're ahead and go on to something else. Don't force the issue. I had a speaking academy and it was very well received and very successful, but it was costing me too much in terms of time. I was able to do more and make more by not continuing on in my speaking academies. I stopped the academy after the best one we had to date. You have time to stop and smell the roses and decide which direction you want to go.

▶ *Join a community:* There is nothing like the support of a community behind you to help you identify and achieve your goals. You see this with people looking to lose weight. Many of the most successful franchises are those with a sense of community behind them, reminding people that they are not alone in their goals. This is also seen in the fitness realm. There are running groups or cycling groups of people with like-minded goals working together and helping each other with tips and tricks that might work for one another. This is also very prevalent in the business world. Join a community, network, work with a coach or mentor, and share your ideas and thoughts with the intent of growing into the next chapter of who you are within your brand or business.

▶ *Stay in the loop:* If you have gained success in one area, don't leave it. Stay in the field, learn from others, and add to it in an overall sense. This is why so many former athletes become sportscasters, do sports radio, or even coach after playing. These are areas that they love, so why wouldn't they want to be a part of the game long term?

You will have to take each new venture and goal with an attitude of what works for you, your lifestyle, time, and intended focus. However, personally, I take on the approach of being humble, setting a bigger goal, working even harder, and ignoring the noise of those not aligned with the target.

CHAPTER 16

The Takeaways

So here we are, at the end of the book and you have successfully learned how to achieve success.

I have not only shared my stories of achieving success, but have also given you the tools you need to create your own successes as well.

So, as a recap, let's identify your Cycle.

AMBITION

What Are Your Realistic Goals?

No one starts at the top. Think realistically. Think about your company, product, service, or brand overall that you are seeking to succeed. What are your short-term and long-term goals?

What would make a difference in helping you achieve those goals? What are your realistic daily goals? What are your realistic one-year goals? What are your realistic five-year goals?

Daily Goals

_____

_____

_____

One-Year Goals

_____

_____

_____

Five-Year Goals

_____

_____

_____

Stepping Outside of the Box

Have you successfully identified areas that you can change to help you grow your brand? Have you considered coaching, mentors, professional development, networking opportunities?

What does stepping out of the box look like for you?

Developing Your Road Map to Success

Do you have a timeline? Do you have a plan? What does your road map look like? You have set these daily goals, one-year goals, and five-year goals. The road map to success is laying out the actions you will take to actually achieve those goals. A goal with no plan of action is just a dream. Are you a dreamer or are you actually going to be successful? Much of that lies in this part. When you set your goals, you focused on being realistic. The road map has to accompany that. Make a road map that you can actually achieve. It will be narrow at first, but as your brand and business grow, the road will widen, and you will have more options. Remember, you will have to detour along the map. Things don't always go according to plan; pivot and keep going.

What does your road map look like to accompany those goals?

Daily Road Map

One-Year Road Map

Five-Year Road Map

_____

_____

_____

DRIVE

*Identify Your **Why***

Regardless of what business or brand you choose to create, it's so important to know your *why*. Why do you want to be successful? It goes past "To become rich." That will not suffice, because once you become rich, then what? You are done? If you are going to put yourself and your family through years of sacrifice and hard work, the *why* has to be bigger than the sacrifice. What is the purpose of your work? Do you know? What do you want to achieve out of your work? What is your mission?

To help you, we established a sentence to complete: "To _____ so that _____."

You have already had time to practice several sentences. Which *why* stood out to you the most? Write it below.

"To _____,

so that _____."

Identify Your Vision

Now that you have your *why,* you are able to vision-cast and time travel yourself into the future. Where are you? What are you doing? Be wild with your vision. Think of Matthew McConaughey's speech where he was constantly chasing his hero, himself ten years down the road. That's vision. Where do you want to be? Earlier, in ambition, we set realistic goals. The vision is the bigger aspect of where you want those goals to ultimately take you. Think of those goals and time travel into the future with each one, creating the vision for each one. This is the time to really understand where you want this to take you overall. Remember John F. Kennedy with his vision to have man walk on the moon. In order to have this crazy vision, he had to assemble the right team to take the steps to achieve it.

So, what is your vision? Take a few moments to time travel and see where you are going with this vision. You may find you are soaring high in one area and maybe not so high in others. When I vision-cast, I found some of my ventures would be "tap outs" and maybe become too much work and take away from other more lucrative opportunities. That's OK. My speaking academy was amazing and very successful, but very time consuming for me. I had to stop it for a while because my vision was so big on other ventures that I was hurting myself in an area that I had already plateaued in. Even your visions have to pivot sometimes.

So, what are your visions for your brand or company? I have a different vision for every venture I have going on, from keynote speaking to consulting, from executive coaching to being a brand ambassador. Identify each leg's vision to understand where you are going.

Motivation vs. Inspiration

We talked about the difference between motivating someone to do something versus inspiring someone to do something. If I motivate you, I'm doing it for selfish reasons, for what I want from you, and I will have to continue to motivate you for every task I want from you. But if I inspire you, I have sparked a rise in your soul to change or want something for yourself, not for what I want from you.

If you lead your team with inspiration versus motivation, you will not only get more done in a timely manner, but you also will not be exhausted having to constantly motivate people to work or want better for themselves.

WORK HARD

It's Not a Nine-To-Five, but a Ninety-Five-Hour Workweek

We have established the idea that you will be working hard. You will work a regular job to pay your bills, and then nights, weekends, and likely holidays too, to create your side hustle. You will sacrifice and you will work harder than you may have ever worked. However, over the years, you will see things start to turn. You will start seeing the fruits of your labor. Your vision will start coming into the picture as you check off the goals along the road map that you created.

However, the reality is this: think about some of your favorite actors, actresses, musicians, and public figures who seem to be everywhere—the truth is they likely "made it" by society's terms a long time ago, but find that they are busier than they have ever been. I think about The Rock, Steve Harvey, and Tony Robbins. All of those guys found success. The Rock became successful when he was in the World Wrestling Federation. Steve Harvey became extremely successful on the Kings of Comedy Tour. Tony Robbins has established himself as *the* keynote speaker of the 21st century. So they should all have nothing but time on their hands, right? Wrong. Each of these people, and many more we could name, has found that he is increasingly working harder the more successful he becomes. Each makes new legs of success. The Rock has a production company, has become a social media influencer, is an actor, has a new tequila line, hosts a TV show, has a deal with Under Armour...the list goes on. Steve Harvey hosts *Family Feud*, *The Steve Harvey Show*, and *Miss America*, performs comedy shows, and executive produces other shows, and so on. Tony Robbins has multiple deals as a brand ambassador for companies, is a keynote speaker, and holds sold-out seminars.

You will likely see that as you succeed, it doesn't mean you are working any less. It will be a different type of work, and you will likely see a bigger monetary gain for your time, but you will continue to work hard.

Focus On You, Not Your Competition

When you are working hard, you will see it's common to want to compare yourself to others. Keep the focus on yourself and your own goals and road map, and don't get sidetracked on what others do or have. I have seen so many times in this business people buy things to impress other people in the business into thinking they have a certain amount of wealth. However, the very same people will be struggling because they are living outside their means to keep up with a certain image. That is all it is, an image. Take the image away. You will one day be able to drive that car you want, buy that house you want, go on those vacations; don't jump the gun.

During this time of working hard, you need to focus more on growing your businesses and brands and less on what it looks like other people are doing.

Build Your Power Team

As you implement everything above, you will start to see the successes show. This is the time when you need to build a team of inspired people around you that understand your *why*, see the vision, and work equally hard.

These people will help elevate your brand to the next level. Rome wasn't built in a day, and it was never built alone. Utilize people with strengths that you don't have and trust them to do their job. However, you must know that as people become a part of your team, if they aren't inspired to create for themselves, don't have the same work ethic as you, or truly don't understand the vision of the brand, then they will likely not be on your team for the long haul. You want your team to be people that will not only assist you and your growth, but also have areas where you can assist them. You are a part of their team as much as they are a part of your team.

The power team will take you further than you could possibly go alone, and in a much faster time.

Multiple Streams of Income

As you have checked off the ambition list and the drive list, and have moved into working hard and establishing your team to help you along the way, you will see things will start to work on their own. You will see your hard work has manifested in a well-oiled machine of success as you find pockets of time becoming available with less of a need for hands-on attention from you. This is when you start to think of another venture. It could be in relation to the one you just found success with or something totally different. It's time to add on. Add a leg to an already functioning service or product. Add on to your résumé of what else you can offer your clients. Or add a different field of study altogether. Again, think back to The Rock, Steve Harvey, and Tony Robbins. The Rock has legs of success that play into a field he has already mastered with his production company, but he also has new creations stemming from his interests. Steve Harvey and Tony Robbins have moved into other areas as well.

What areas of your current Success Cycle project could you branch out on to create another line of income? Could you add a leg to an already functioning and self-producing avenue? Or do you have an interest that you would like to explore into a successful product or service? Be mindful when you are in the cycle of what other options to add later, but get one area of expertise in full motion before adding another. Develop those multiple streams of income to provide options for yourself and your family.

REPEAT THE CYLE

Set New Goals

The Cycle never finishes. When you find your brand, company, or service in a place of success, set new goals. It may be with the same Cycle or a new one. Don't become complacent. That will be the end of your company, much like it was for my construction company. Repeat the Cycle. Take it to another level or create a new leg. Maybe your company or brand has done well but could be better—start over. Maybe it's running well on its own and you want to start a different venture—start over. The Cycle works for new and existing plans. The very same Cycle I developed in my office years ago with poster boards decorating the walls is the same Cycle I use today with over ten different money-producing plans in motion. It's the same Cycle my power team uses for their personal projects as well as our joint ones. It is the same Cycle that will bring your thoughts and ideas into real-life successes.

About the Author

Marques Ogden is a former NFL athlete who is originally from Washington DC. He was raised by a single father, who taught him and his brother Jonathan about the importance of ambition, drive, and hard work. After his NFL career he started a construction business, and grew it into one of the largest minority subcontracting businesses in the city of Baltimore. After making a bad mistake, Marques had to file a chapter 7 bankruptcy. Today, Marques is an inspirational keynote speaker, executive coach, and business leader. He is married to his wife Bonnie, and has two beautiful daughters, Ava and Farrah.